# DATE DUE

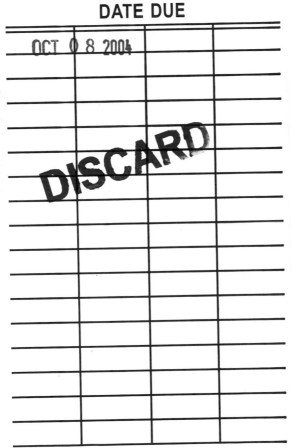

Understanding

# The Scarlet
# Letter

New and future titles in the Understanding Great Literature
series include:

Understanding *The Catcher in the Rye*
Understanding *Flowers for Algernon*
Understanding *Hamlet*
Understanding *I Am the Cheese*
Understanding *Johnny Tremain*
Understanding *Macbeth*
Understanding *Of Mice and Men*
Understanding *The Outsiders*
Understanding *Romeo and Juliet*
Understanding *The Yearling*

# The Scarlet Letter

UNDERSTANDING GREAT LITERATURE

Clarice Swisher

LUCENT
BOOKS ®

THOMSON
™
GALE

San Diego • Detroit • New York • San Francisco • Cleveland
New Haven, Conn. • Waterville, Maine • London • Munich

# THOMSON
★
## GALE

*For Angela and Nicole*

© 2003 by Lucent Books. Lucent Books is an imprint of The Gale Group, Inc., a division of Thomson Learning, Inc.

Lucent Books® and Thomson Learning™ are trademarks used herein under license.

*For more information, contact*
Lucent Books
27500 Drake Rd.
Farmington Hills, MI 48331-3535
Or you can visit our Internet site at http://www.gale.com

### LIBRARY OF CONGRESS CATALOGING-IN-PUBLICATION DATA

Swisher, Clarice, 1933–
  Understanding *The Scarlet Letter* / by Clarice Swisher.
  p. cm. — (Understanding Great Literature)
Summary: Discusses the life of Nathaniel Hawthorne and the historical context, plot, themes, characters, and literary analysis of his novel *The Scarlet Letter*.
Includes bibliographical references and index.
    ISBN 1-56006-812-4 (hardback : alk. paper)
    1. Hawthorne, Nathaniel, 1804–1864. Scarlet letter—Juvenile literature. 2. Historical fiction, American—History and criticism—Juvenile literature. [1. Hawthorne, Nathaniel, 1804—1864. Scarlet letter. 2. American literature—History and criticism.] I. Title. II. Series.
    PS1868 .S95 2003
    813' .3—dc21

                                                                    2001007840

Printed in the United States of America

# Contents

# FOREWORD

"Except for a living man, there is nothing more wonderful than a book!" wrote the widely respected nineteenth-century teacher and writer Charles Kingsley. A book, he continued, "is a message to us from human souls we never saw. And yet these [books] arouse us, terrify us, teach us, comfort us, open our hearts to us as brothers." There are many different kinds of books, of course; and Kingsley was referring mainly to those containing literature—novels, plays, short stories, poems, and so on. In particular, he had in mind those works of literature that were and remain widely popular with readers of all ages and from many walks of life.

Such popularity might be based on one or several factors. On the one hand, a book might be read and studied by people in generation after generation because it is a literary classic, with characters and themes of universal relevance and appeal. Homer's epic poems, the *Iliad* and the *Odyssey*, Chaucer's *Canterbury Tales*, Shakespeare's *Hamlet* and *Romeo and Juliet*, and Dickens's *A Christmas Carol* fall into this category. Some popular books, on the other hand, are more controversial. Mark Twain's *Huckleberry Finn* and J. D. Salinger's *The Catcher in the Rye*, for instance, have their legions of devoted fans who see them as great literature; while others view them as less than worthy because of their racial depictions, profanity, or other factors.

Still another category of popular literature includes realistic modern fiction, including novels such as Robert Cormier's *I Am the Cheese* and S.E. Hinton's *The Outsiders*. Their keen social insights and sharp character portrayals have consistently reached out to and captured the imaginations of many teenagers and young adults; and for this reason they are often assigned and studied in schools.

These and other similar works have become the "old standards" of the literary scene. They are the ones that people most often read, discuss, and study; and each has, by virtue of its content, critical success, or just plain longevity, earned the right to be the subject of a book examining its content. (Some, of course, like the *Iliad* and *Hamlet*, have been the subjects of numerous books already; but their literary stature is so lofty that there can never be too many books about them!) For millions of readers and students in one generation after another, each of these works becomes, in a sense, an adventure in appreciation, enjoyment, and learning.

The main purpose of Lucent's Understanding Great Literature series is to aid the reader in that ongoing literary adventure. Each volume in the series focuses on a single literary work that a majority of critics and teachers view as a classic and/or that is widely studied and discussed in schools. A typical volume first tells why the work in question is important. Then follow detailed overviews of the author's life, the work's historical background, its plot, its characters, and its themes. Numerous quotes from the work, as well as by critics and other experts, are interspersed throughout and carefully documented with footnotes for those who wish to pursue further research. Also included is a list of ideas for essays and other student projects relating to the work, an appendix of literary criticisms and analyses by noted scholars, and a comprehensive annotated bibliography.

The great nineteenth-century American poet Henry David Thoreau once quipped: "Read the best books first, or you may not have a chance to read them at all." For those who are reading or about to read the "best books" in the literary canon, the comprehensive, thorough, and thoughtful volumes of the Understanding Great Literature series are indispensable guides and sources of enrichment.

# America's First Great Novelist

B y writing *The Scarlet Letter*, Nathaniel Hawthorne achieved many firsts in American literature. It is the first novel to make extensive use of symbolism, the first fictional exposé of Puritan life, and the first novel with a woman in a heroic role. For a century and a half its themes and artistic qualities have absorbed countless readers.

*The Scarlet Letter* "has become an acknowledged masterpiece of modern literature," according to editors Sculley Bradley, Richmond Croom Beatty, and E. Hudson Long in *The American Tradition in Literature*.[1] Perhaps the reason Hawthorne's novel is considered a masterpiece is that it contains truths that resonate with readers generation after generation regardless of their circumstances. Hawthorne intended for the reader to contemplate large issues such as the nature of sin, moral authority, and the consequences of wrongdoing. Though the world today is vastly different from Puritan New England, the issues of guilt, shame, and morality belong to every generation and every culture.

Hawthorne wrote *The Scarlet Letter* during what is known as literature's Romantic Period. In their works, Romantic writers in America and Europe emphasized imagination, personal freedom, and the mystery of remote times and places. Moreover, they sought to glorify nature and promote optimism and idealism. Though Hawthorne wrote many romantic short stories, he took a different direction with *The Scarlet Letter*, calling it a psychological romance. Personally, he saw the world with a less optimistic view than many of his Romantic contemporaries. In *The Scarlet Letter*, Hawthorne chose to focus on complex issues of the human heart and soul. The historical record he found while working in the customhouse, the record of a woman forced to wear a scarlet letter as a punishment for adultery, offered him the vehicle for calling attention to these issues. The result is a novel that combines romantic qualities with psychological insight.

Hawthorne used symbols extensively to provide the psychological dimension. As one scholar notes, "Hawthorne employed a continuous system of symbolic suggestion, which clarified the 'larger meanings' beyond the power of immediate action or dialogue."[2] He guided the reader toward his symbols. For example, in referring to the weeds growing on the grave in the cemetery and the rosebush by the prison, Hawthorne uses words like "typify" and "symbolize" to alert the reader to connect these common objects with larger meanings. On several occasions, descriptions of physical phenomena suggest emotional experience, as in the forest scene when the sun bursts forth on Hester and Dimmesdale emphasizing their joy. Throughout the novel, Hawthorne directs the reader to interpret symbols that reflect inward reality.

Hawthorne's novel, set in Puritan New England, gives the reader a historically accurate vision of early America. Though a portrayal of cultural history is not the main purpose of *The Scarlet Letter*, the novel is the first fictional account of Puritan life. Hawthorne incorporates historical figures as characters, such as Governor Bellingham, Governor Winthrop, and Mistress Hibbins. He portrays the members of the community authentically both in their ideas and in their customs. The election day holiday, the day the new governor was to be installed, is historical. Critics Randall Stewart and Dorothy

*Nathaniel Hawthorne, author of* The Scarlet Letter.

Bethurum say, "More truly than any other book in American literature, *The Scarlet Letter* embodies Puritan ideals and the Puritan way of life."[3]

Though Hester Prynne was a real person who lived in Puritan New England and was forced to wear a scarlet letter, Hawthorne's Hester is given a central, heroic role that is fictional. On one hand, Hawthorne makes Hester admirable: able to cope with her punishment and able to use intelligence and determination to endure her isolation and humiliation at the community's hands. Hester is heroic in that she never abdicates her responsibility to her child nor her love for Dimmesdale, and when she sees Chillingworth's injustice, she has the courage to act. On the other hand, Hawthorne also makes Hester an object of pity, denied the opportunity to experience joy and passion. She is the victim of laws made by men. Critic Maxwell Geismar says that one of the things that makes *The Scarlet Letter* so impressive today is "the brooding note of pity with which Hawthorne viewed those heroic women who were sacrificed, whether by sacred edict or social convenience, on the altar of masculine institutions."[4] Without self-pity, without bitterness, without rancor, Hester stands tall with an independent spirit—an authentic American heroine.

Hawthorne's artistry is evident in four significant ways. First, he creates vivid pictures complete with color and shades of light

*Actress Demi Moore brought* The Scarlet Letter *to new audiences with her portrayal of Hester Prynne in the 1995 film version of the novel.*

and dark. So striking is Hawthorne's visual imagery that one critic said that *The Scarlet Letter* is all pictures—still life and action scenes. Second, the novel has a clear structure: three scaffold scenes placed at the beginning, middle, and end, framed by the opening customhouse essay and the conclusion. Critic Leland Schubert says, "The structural plan of *The Scarlet Letter* is one of its most beautiful and artistic qualities."[5] Third, Hawthorne uses irony to create constant suspense and tension. Critic Richard Harter Fogle observes: "The intensity of *The Scarlet Letter* comes in part from a sustained and rigorous dramatic irony. This irony arises naturally from the theme of 'secret sin,' or concealment."[6] For example, the townspeople idolize Dimmesdale, but have no idea that he is Pearl's father. Finally, Hawthorne makes skillful use of the narrator's voice. Critic Alison Easton explains how the narrator's voice works: "He is one of the many strands of the novel, out of which is spun a web of confrontations, questions, and doubts. His descriptions always tend to slide into multiple interpretations."[7]

Critics have had a century and a half to analyze *The Scarlet Letter*. The majority of them concur that it is a complex novel worthy of being studied by each new generation of readers. It fascinates readers because it has suspense, and the story raises questions about the human soul. Readers study Hawthorne's symbols and suggestions in search of their answers to Hawthorne's psychological questions.

# CHAPTER ONE

# The Life of Nathaniel Hawthorne

Nathaniel Hawthorne was born on the fourth of July, 1804, in Salem, Massachusetts, the second child of Captain Nathaniel and Elizabeth Hathorne. (Hawthorne later inserted the "w" into his name.) The couple had two other children: Elizabeth, born in 1802, and Maria Louisa, born in 1808. Captain Hathorne was a merchant seaman, away from home for many months of the year. When Hawthorne was four years old his father died from yellow fever on a voyage to the Caribbean. At the time, Nathaniel, his mother, and his sisters lived with Captain Hathorne's parents, but they soon moved to the home of the Mannings, Elizabeth's parents and her eight brothers and sisters.

## Influence of the Mannings and Hawthornes

Nathaniel's maternal grandfather, Richard Manning, was a successful businessman. After Richard Manning died, Nathaniel's Uncle Robert became his guardian. Robert Manning expected Nathaniel to comply with rules and learn the practical tasks of earning a living, while his aunts and other uncles fostered his intellectual, literary, and artistic interests. Nathaniel, who had a sensitive nature, resented Robert's attempts to direct his life, but he never rebelled outwardly and assumed that he too would one day enter the family business. In her book *Family Themes and Hawthorne's Fiction: The Tenacious Web*, Gloria C. Erlich comments on the effect of Robert's harsh ways: "Nathaniel's passivity and indolence appeared especially unmanly in the presence of Robert Manning's energetic capabilities, not only to the uncle but to the boy himself. The resulting self-distrust was to be permanently in conflict with Hawthorne's innate pride."[8]

In spite of Robert Manning's efforts Nathaniel's sensitive nature and artistic interests remained dominant in his personality. When he was a young boy he began reading poetry, adventure and mystery stories, and colonial history. In part this was because at the age of nine he injured his foot playing ball, an injury that kept him inactive for three years.

By 1816 his lameness had improved, and Nathaniel, his sisters, and his mother, to get away from the crowded Manning household, moved to Raymond, Maine, to live in one of the Manning houses on the shore of Lake Sebago. There Nathaniel spent three idyllic years roaming in the woods and fishing on the lake. In his biography of Hawthorne, Randall Stewart says, "Hawthorne was later to regard the Raymond years as the happiest of his life; he often told his family and friends of this glorious epoch when, as he expressed it, he 'lived like a bird of the air.'"[9] Then, in 1818,

*Nathaniel Hawthorne was born in this house in Salem, Massachusetts.*

the Mannings brought Hawthorne back to Salem to prepare for college. Living again under the influence of his Uncle Robert, he kept books for the Manning stagecoach lines for a salary of one dollar a week. Nathaniel was uninterested in the family business, however, and by the age of seventeen, he knew he wanted to be a writer. In the spring of 1821 he approached the subject of his profession in a letter to his mother, who was still in Maine. With an element of humor, he wrote:

> I have not yet concluded what profession I shall have. The being a Minister is of course out of the Question. I should not think that even you could desire me to choose so dull a way of life. . . . As to Lawyers there are so many of them already that one half of them (upon a moderate calculation) are in a state of actual starvation. A Physician seems to be Hobson's choice, but yet I should not like to live by the diseases and infirmities of my fellow creatures. And it would weigh very heavily on my conscience if in the course of my practice, I should chance to send any unlucky patient "ad inferum," which being interpreted, is "to the realms below." . . . What do you think of my becoming an author, and relying for support upon my pen?[10]

Nathaniel kept his goal a secret from others and followed his uncle's plan for him to study at Bowdoin College.

## Hawthorne's College Years

In 1821 Hawthorne entered Bowdoin College in New Brunswick, Maine. He quickly settled into the college's rigorous curriculum of Latin, Greek, mathematics, philosophy, English composition, and natural science. While he did poorly in metaphysics and mathematics, Hawthorne excelled in Latin and English. In his book titled *Hawthorne*, biographer Newton Arvin reports "Professor Packard remembered his [Hawthorne's] Latin prose exercises for the rest of a long lifetime; and it is said that Professor Newman had so high a regard for his talents in English composition that he fell into the habit of reading Hawthorne's themes aloud to his assembled family."[11]

Hawthorne enjoyed both the intellectual and social activities of college life. He joined a literary society, where he made lifelong friends—future poet Henry Wadsworth Longfellow, future

*Nathaniel Hawthorne attended Bowdoin College, in New Brunswick, Maine, from 1821 to 1825.*

U.S. President Franklin Pierce, and Horatio Bridge, future literary critic and Hawthorne supporter. After four years at Bowdoin, Hawthorne graduated in 1825, eighteenth in a class of thirty-eight.

## Back to Salem and a Life of Solitude

By the time Hawthorne graduated from college, his mother and sisters had left Maine and moved to Salem, Massachusetts, and he moved in with them. His mother's quiet house in Salem was the ideal place for him to think and reflect, to read widely, and to practice the craft of writing. For twelve years, from 1825 to 1837, Hawthorne prepared his mind and developed his skills. He studied his Puritan past. In addition to acquiring factual knowledge, Hawthorne reflected and daydreamed about Puritan New England until he felt he had absorbed the way of life and thinking of the colony.

Hawthorne spent even more time writing than he spent reading during those twelve years. He wrote historical sketches, allegorical tales, and one novel. These early efforts failed to bring him an income, however. Finding no publisher for his first collection of tales, he tossed them into the fire. In 1828 he published his novel *Fanshawe* anonymously at his own expense, but reviewers and critics paid no attention to it. Soon after its publication, Hawthorne came to dislike it himself. In *Nathaniel Hawthorne: A Biography*, Arlin Turner explains: "He had overlooked one lesson he might have learned from them [his favorite British writers], particularly from Scott: the value of place and history in fiction. Even in *Fanshawe* he had not achieved full reality of place and time. He now recognized a need to know the land, the people, and the history of the region of his fiction as intimately as Scott knew the Highlands."[12]

Eventually, Hawthorne achieved some success with his tales. The first was "The Hollow of the Three Hills," published by the *Salem Gazette* in 1830. Once again Hawthorne tried to sell a collection of tales. Again he found no publisher, so he sent the collection to Samuel G. Goodrich, editor of *Token*, an annual gift book. Goodrich was interested only in individual stories and between 1831 and 1837 published twenty-two of Hawthorne's tales under a pseudonym. Hawthorne also sold eight stories to the *New England Magazine* in 1835, all of which were published anonymously. Still, his success did not translate into monetary rewards. In 1836, in a letter to his friend from college, Horatio Bridge, Hawthorne said that he could earn no more than three hundred dollars a year selling stories to magazines and annual gift books.

Bridge advised Hawthorne to prepare a collection of his best tales and publish them under his own name. Hawthorne took Bridge's advice and selected eighteen previously published stories, titled the collection *Twice-Told Tales*, and submitted them to Goodrich. This time Goodrich agreed to publish the collection. Without Hawthorne's knowledge, Bridge had guaranteed Goodrich two hundred and fifty dollars to offset losses he might incur in publishing the collection. *Twice-Told Tales* was published in March 1837. Its immediate critical attention—two favorable reviews and a third glowing review by his college friend Henry Wadsworth Longfellow—encouraged Hawthorne, although he still received little money for his efforts.

## Travels Beyond Salem

During his twelve years in Salem, Hawthorne interrupted his studies to travel around New England with his uncle, Samuel Manning, who searched every summer for horses for the Manning stagecoach lines. During these trips Hawthorne recorded in his journal images of people and places and saved the journal for later use. Critic Randall Stewart says of Hawthorne's travels:

By his travels over New England, he was recreating his mind, enlarging his knowledge of human nature, and gathering impressions which could be used in his writings (was making himself indeed the chief literary authority in New England life and manners). Recognition was slow, but the appearance of the *Twice-Told Tales* in 1837 was the beginning of an enduring reputation.[13]

*By 1851 Nathaniel Hawthorne had become a prolific writer, having sold numerous stories to a variety of New England literary magazines.*

Following the publication of *Twice-Told Tales*, Hawthorne began a run of successes with his writing. By 1845 he had sold twenty-two stories to the *Democratic Review*, which paid him between three and five dollars per page, and he had sold nine stories to other literary magazines.

In the meantime, following brief trips to visit his friend Bridge in Maine and to North Adams, Massachusetts, Hawthorne returned to Salem in late 1838. There he met Sophia Peabody, daughter of a Salem dentist. Although Sophia was sickly, an invalid who had suffered headaches for many years, she was also beautiful and talented. Sophia was educated in Latin, Greek, and Hebrew and had talent in drawing and painting. She contributed to Hawthorne's work a sketch of Ilbrahim, the child in Hawthorne's story "The Gentle Boy." Hawthorne was charmed by her, and by the end of the year, the couple was engaged.

Before he and Sophia could be married, however, Hawthorne needed to earn more money than his writing was paying him. Using political connections, in 1839 Hawthorne got a job as a weigher and gauger of salt and coal at the Boston Custom House. He was happy to earn an annual salary of fifteen hundred dollars a year, but he disliked being separated from Sophia. To quell his loneliness, he spent his evenings writing letters to her. In one he expresses both his longing for Sophia and his respect for her:

"Belovedest— . . . I sometimes wish that thou couldst be with me on board my salt-vessels and colliers, because there are many things of which thou mightst make such pretty descriptions; and in future years, when thy husband is again busy at the loom of fiction, he would weave in these little pictures."[14]

In January 1841 Hawthorne resigned from his job at the Boston Custom House. He spent the next few months living at Brook Farm, an experimental cooperative living project located nine miles west of Boston in West Roxbury. Hawthorne had invested a thousand dollars in the project in hopes of earning additional income. He worked there tending animals and farming crops until August, when he saw that the experiment was a financial failure. Moreover, he found that the farmwork disrupted his writing.

## Marriage and Old Manse

After three years, Hawthorne's efforts to save enough money to wed Sophia had largely failed, but the couple decided to marry anyway. On July 7, 1842, Hawthorne and Sophia were married at the home of Sophia's parents, who had moved to Boston. The couple rented a home known as Old Manse in Concord. Their first child Una, a girl, was born there in March 1844. The Hawthornes spent four happy years at Old Manse, years they cherished for the solitude it afforded them. Biographer Gloria C. Erlich explains the success of the Hawthornes's marriage: "The marriage was beneficial for both partners. It gave Hawthorne intimate human contact and links to normal human experience. It led Sophia from chronic invalidism into sufficient health for motherhood and a fairly long, active life. With it, both found a satisfying and enduring physical relationship that made their separations hard to endure."[15]

Hawthorne had been writing and publishing steadily since he left his mother's house in 1838. In addition to his journals and tales, he wrote children's books. *Grandfather's Chair*, 1841, a children's history of New England through the Revolutionary War, was a success. His other children's books from this period were *Famous Old People* and *Liberty Tree*, both published in 1841, and *Biographical Stories for Children*, published in 1842. He published a new enlarged edition of *Twice-Told Tales* in 1842 and in 1846 *Mosses from an Old Manse*, a collection of twenty-

*Nathaniel Hawthorne and his wife Sophia moved into this house, known as Old Manse, in Concord, Massachusetts, shortly after their wedding in 1842.*

three pieces, seventeen of which he had written while living at Old Manse.

## Salem Again and the Custom House

The Hawthornes left Old Manse in 1845 and moved to his mother's house in Salem because Hawthorne hoped to receive another political appointment, once again in order to supplement his writing income. On April 3, 1846, President James Polk appointed Hawthorne to a post at the Salem Custom House at a salary of twelve hundred dollars per year.

In June that same year, Hawthorne's son, Julian, was born. Hawthorne and Sophia were happy with each other and enjoyed their role as parents. However, when Zachary Taylor, a Whig, won the 1848 presidential election, and because customhouse jobs were strictly political appointments, Hawthorne, a Democrat, lost his post. Hawthorne was angry and worried about how he could support his wife and two children. Yet his wife remained supportive. When he first told Sophia about losing his job, she reportedly said that now he could write the novel he had been planning, *The Scarlet Letter*. Then she brought out money she had saved from the household allowances.

While Hawthorne was still coping with the loss of a job, his mother became gravely ill and, within a few days, died on July 31, 1849. Contrasting the youth of his daughter with the last days of his mother's life, Hawthorne wrote in his journal on July 29:

*In September 1849, four years after moving his family into this home in Salem, Massachusetts, Hawthorne began writing* The Scarlet Letter.

For a long time I knelt there, holding her hand; and surely it is the darkest hour I ever lived. Afterwards I stood by the open window and looked through the crevice of the curtain. The shouts, laughter, and cries of the two children had come up into the chamber from the open air, making a strange contrast with the death-bed scene. And now, through the crevice of the curtain, I saw my little Una of the golden locks, looking very beautiful, and so full of spirit and life that she was life itself. And then I looked at my poor dying mother, and seemed to see the whole of human existence at once, standing in the dusty midst of it. Oh, what a mockery, if what I saw were all—let the interval between youth and dying age be filled up with what happiness it might![16]

His sadness and worry did not, however, keep Hawthorne from writing. By September 24 he had begun working on *The Scarlet Letter*, a story based on a diary and a worn piece of fabric in the shape of a capital A that Hawthorne had discovered stored in the customhouse. In his introductory essay to *The Scarlet Letter*, "The Custom House," Hawthorne describes his find:

> But the object that most drew my attention, in the mysterious package, was a certain affair of fine red cloth, much worn and faded. There were traces about it of gold embroidery, which, however, was greatly frayed and defaced; so that none, or very little, of the glitter was left. It had been wrought, as was easy to perceive, with wonderful skill of needlework. . . . This rag of scarlet cloth,—for time, and wear, and a sacrilegious moth, had reduced it to little other than a rag,—on careful examination, assumed the shape of a letter. It was the capital letter A.[17]

*The Custom House in Salem, Massachusetts, where Nathaniel Hawthorne worked from 1846 to 1848.*

Hawthorne worked sometimes nine hours a day on his novel, completing the whole book in six months. *The Scarlet Letter* was published in Boston on March 16, 1850, and published in England soon after. It sold six thousand copies in America and received high praise from the critics, except for a few who thought the tone was gloomy and theme of adultery immoral. Most critics also liked the opening essay's humorous account of the local customhouse, although Salem residents were outraged at what they felt was Hawthorne's insulting portrayal of their town.

## Lenox

With his own literary reputation established and with Salem residents angry with him, Hawthorne and his family moved in May 1850 to Lenox, a peaceful village in western Massachusetts. Arvin notes that Hawthorne rented "A little frame house painted red—Hawthorne called it, dutifully, "the Scarlet Letter"—with its southern windows looking out over the waters of Stockbridge Bowl and at the smooth and placid slopes of Monument Mountain beyond."[18] Hawthorne could now relax and enjoy gardening, building, fishing, and playing with his children.

The year and a half that Hawthorne lived in Lenox was a productive time for him. He completed *The House of Seven Gables*, a novel about the mysterious events in the lives of the Pyncheon family, in January 1851, and it was published in April. The novel was received with greater enthusiasm in America than *The Scarlet Letter* had been and was even more popular in England. Next came *A Wonder Book*, a children's book of tales based on Greek myths. Turner describes Hawthorne's attitude about this children's book: "He took satisfaction in the book and . . . said that 'it seemed to reach a higher point, in its own way,' than anything he had written 'for grown people.' He was pleased to have reviewers speak of the sunny and happy quality of the book, and to have proved that he could adapt myths for children without writing down to them."[19]

Then he wrote a new preface for the third edition of *Twice-Told Tales*, as well as a preface for another collection, *The Snow Image and Other Twice-Told Tales*. This volume included four stories written after *Mosses from an Old Manse*—"The Snow Image," "The Great Stone Face," "Main Street," and "Ethan

Brand." The other seven tales in this collection were ones he had passed over when selecting stories for *Twice-Told Tales.*

## Wayside

After this productive period, Hawthorne's attention turned to new events. In May 1851 his third child, Rose, was born. By fall he was tiring of Lenox and longing to be nearer to the sea and the city streets. On November 21, 1851, Hawthorne and his family left Lenox and moved to Wayside, a home in Concord that sat on nine acres of land. Turner describes the satisfaction of the family's return to Concord.

> In a few weeks the Hawthornes were fully restored to the community they had left almost seven years earlier. . . . Sophia's letters to her mother reflect genuine delight at the return to familiar scenes and old friends at Concord. Her assessment of the Concord neighbors may have been more favorable than her husband's, but he had indicated a genuine satisfaction from the time he purchased the house, which he said had "picturesque capabilities."[20]

From this house the happy family enjoyed walks to their former home, Old Manse.

*Wayside, the Hawthornes's Concord, Massachusetts, home. The family was happy to return to Concord after a seven-year absence.*

*Franklin Pierce,*
*Hawthorne's college friend,*
*became president of the*
*United States in 1853.*

At Wayside Hawthorne was busy writing. He wrote *Blithedale Romance,* a novel about his experiences at Brook Farm ten years earlier. It was published in America on July 14, 1852, and shortly after in London, but the reading public was less enthusiastic about this book than they had been about either *The Scarlet Letter* or *The House of Seven Gables.* Though he was disappointed by the poor reception, his confidence as a novelist was unshaken.

By June 1852 Hawthorne's college friend Franklin Pierce had won the Democratic nomination for President. Having offered to help Pierce's election effort, Hawthorne wrote a biography of Pierce, which would be used for publicity. Hawthorne wanted Pierce to win the election and offer him an appointment in England. Hawthorne's plan was to visit the homeland of his ancestors and travel to scenes described in English literature, a trip he could not afford to pay for personally. Pierce did win, and he did appoint Hawthorne to a position as consul in Liverpool, England. Before departing, Hawthorne wrote *Tanglewood Tales,* another retelling of Greek myths for children, which was published in America and England in 1853.

## The Hawthornes in England

The Hawthornes sailed from Boston for Liverpool on July 6, 1853, on the steamer *Niagra.* Hawthorne began work on August 1 in an office near the Liverpool docks. His job as consul consisted of keeping accounts, processing documents, and listening to the complaints of American sailors who claimed they had been mistreated on ships that docked in Liverpool. Hawthorne disliked the work, but he performed his duties well in the tradition taught him years earlier by his uncle, Robert Manning. While in England, preoccupied with his duties as consul, Hawthorne wrote little, producing only *The English Notebook.*

When Hawthorne's consulship ended in 1857, he and his family stayed on, sightseeing around England. They visited Shakespeare's home county of Warwickshire, the Lake District where poet William Wordsworth had lived, London, the Scottish Highlands, and many other places. Hawthorne delighted in his time in England, writing from London, "It is singular, that I feel more at home and familiar there than even in Boston, or in old Salem itself."[21]

When the family left England, they traveled to Paris for sightseeing before going to Rome, the place that Sophia had dreamed of visiting.

## The Hawthornes in Italy

The Hawthornes spent more than a year in Italy, long enough for leisurely sightseeing and for Hawthorne to write extensively in his journal describing people he met and places he visited. In Rome Hawthorne discovered an American artists' colony. Though interested in their art, Hawthorne was more interested in studying the personalities of the residents themselves. One of the artists, Maria Louise Lander of Salem, became the basis for Hilda, a character in *The Marble Faun*, the novel he began writing in Italy. Except for an eight-day sightseeing trip to Florence, the Hawthornes stayed in Rome until 1859, when they left for home.

The Hawthornes planned a brief stop in England before they returned to America, but when they got to London, the London publishers Smith and Elder offered Hawthorne £600 for a new romance, an offer Hawthorne accepted. Since he had started a draft of *The Marble Faun* in Italy, he went to York in the north of England on July 26, 1859, to finish it. The book was published on February 28, 1860, under the title *Transformations*. It came out in Boston a few days later as *The Marble Faun* and received only mediocre reviews.

## The Last Years

Hawthorne and his family finally sailed for America from Liverpool on June 16, 1860, on the steamship *Europa*. The Hawthornes arrived at Wayside in Concord to a warm welcome after an absence of seven years. Gradually Hawthorne returned to writing, using his English notebooks as a basis for magazine pieces. In 1863 he published *Our Old Home*, a collection of sketches drawn from his observations and experiences in England. He made four attempts to

*This twentieth-century photograph depicts Nathaniel Hawthorne's George Street home in London, England, where he spent several years following his appointment as a consul by President Pierce.*

write another novel, but he was unable to work out his complicated plot and themes to his satisfaction. As the year progressed, Hawthorne became weak, sick, and depressed and could no longer write, but he refused to see a doctor.

In May 1864, even though he was not feeling well, Hawthorne went on a trip with Franklin Pierce, whose wife had died a year earlier and who needed the support of a friend. They met in Boston and boarded a train, planning stops on the way to Concord, New Hampshire, Pierce's home. On May 18 they stopped in Plymouth, New Hampshire. Between three and four in the morning of May 19 Pierce went to Hawthorne's room to check on him and found Hawthorne dead. He would have been sixty years old on July 4, 1864. He was buried on May 25 in Concord, Massachusetts.

In the decades following his death, critics largely agreed that Hawthorne's literary career had climaxed with the publication of *The Scarlet Letter.* Though his tales and other novels warrant critical interest, his legacy as an American writer was established with his psychological romance of the scarlet A. In this novel he displays his compassion for people, his deep understanding of the psychological effects of sin and wrongdoing, and his craft as an artist.

⤚

# CHAPTER TWO

# Historical Background for *The Scarlet Letter*

Nathaniel Hawthorne's first novel, *The Scarlet Letter,* was published in 1850, but it is set nearly two hundred years earlier in Puritan New England. His choice of that setting was not a casual one. Hawthorne studied the philosophy and spirit of Puritanism after he had discovered that his ancestors had played important roles in the early history of New England; his understanding of that period is incorporated into the novel.

## Puritan New England

Early settlers brought to New England a worldview based on their reading of the Bible. They thought the Bible contained a complete body of laws that covered ethics, proper dress, marriages, judicial procedures, and all other elements of life. They thought that scripture was in harmony with human reason and that the two—scripture and reason—were a sufficient guide to the whole of life. In the introduction to *American Poetry and Prose,* editor Norman Foerster writes:

> Having come to America as to a promised land, the Puritans soon developed the concept of a Holy Commonwealth, a theocracy, a social organization centering on the churches and their ministers. The more this corporate blessedness was

subverted by Satan—acting through the Indians, the witches, and the internal conflicts of the churches—the more passionately was it believed in and propagated.[22]

The Puritan townspeople in Hawthorne's novel act in accordance with these beliefs. In her introductory essay to *The Scarlet Letter,* Monika Elbert explains that Hawthorne uses the setting of Puritan New England to show that "an individual or a nation cannot escape the past," that "the Puritans carried the vices of the Old World with them into the New World."[23]

## The American Romantic Period

Because Hawthorne had studied the New England of his ancestors but lived two hundred years later during the Romantic Period, *The Scarlet Letter* reflects the ideas of both periods. The Puritan community and its ministers convey Puritan culture and ideals through the plot and dialogue. Hawthorne conveys romantic ideas in more subtle ways. American Romanticism expresses the themes of individualism, self-realization, humanitarianism, and idealism. These themes are evident in the novel, but in reverse: Hawthorne expresses sadness that Hester is denied access to all of these qualities.

Romantic writers focused on the past, stressed imagination, and conveyed a sense of optimism. Hawthorne incorporates ro-

*New England Puritans accompany a minister to church. Puritan ideals, conveyed through the plot and dialogue, are a major feature of* The Scarlet Letter.

*Hawthorne incorporated Romanticism in* The Scarlet Letter *through his use of mysterious characters and a historical setting.*

manticism into the novel through the historical setting and the mystery of Mistress Hibbins's supernatural knowledge and her association with the Black Man in the forest. Hawthorne's writing was far less optimistic than that of his fellow Romantics, due to guilt from his Puritan past and a clear awareness of the dark side of human nature.

## Hawthorne Collects Ideas and Material for His Stories

Since Hawthorne determined at the age of seventeen that he wanted to be a writer, he prepared for his career by recording thoughts, reflections, and observations in his journals over many years. When he began writing *The Scarlet Letter* he had many journal entries from which to draw in creating characters, plot, and themes.

Hawthorne's journal entries make it clear that he had long been thinking about the characters he would later create. For example, anticipating Chillingworth, in 1836 Hawthorne wrote, "To show the effect of gratified revenge. . . . At last, when the miserable victim were utterly trodden down, the triumpher would have become a very devil of evil passions."[24] Hawthorne also recorded ideas for a character like Dimmesdale. For example, Hawthorne referred to a character who was false and miserable, as Dimmesdale was.

The first indication that Hawthorne was formulating a plot involving the scarlet letter dates back to 1837. In *The Yellow Ruff & The Scarlet Letter,* Alfred S. Reid says, "It is generally assumed that a story on the scarlet letter began to germinate in Hawthorne's mind about 1837, some twelve years before *The Scarlet Letter* was finished. For in that year he briefly described in 'Endicott and the Red Cross' a beautiful woman wearing a red letter A sewed to her garment in token of her having committed adultery."[25] In journal entries, Hawthorne refers to the woman who had in fact worn the letter A because she had violated a 1636 law stating that those guilty of adultery must wear two As sewn on their garments.

Journal entries suggest that Hawthorne had long thought about character and plot ideas. He also knew what themes he wanted to portray, based on a pragmatic view of the universe that recognized potential for wrongdoing in human nature. Still, he was able to maintain compassion for fellow humans. According to Turner, "He could accept the universe and see that man, in his proper course, would hold to his ideals, choose among possibilities, and accept the inevitable. This outlook allowed him, or required him, to feel enveloping sympathy—sympathy for both the agents of evil and their victims."[26] With years of reflection in his mind, with an extensive journal, and with confidence in his vision of human nature, Hawthorne was well prepared to write *The Scarlet Letter.*

## Unexpected Events Spark Him to Write

When Hawthorne moved back to Salem in 1845 the prospects for writing a great novel looked dim. Full-time employment at the customhouse left him little time to concentrate on writing. Two events happened coincidentally in 1849, however, to change his circumstances. In the storage facilities in the customhouse, Hawthorne found the historical record of Hester Prynne, the New England woman punished for adultery by being forced to wear a scarlet A on her garment. With this record, he found the faded and tattered remnants of the letter itself. This discovery sparked his imagination. Arvin explains:

> Now, the scarlet "A", if he had ever wholly forgotten it, rekindled itself in his imagination with a new and hotter radiance. For how deep a wrong might it not be the expiation, and of how terrible a loneliness the cause! And what if there might be a wrong greater than that which this woman had done, and a more awful punishment than hers? What if the scarlet letter might appear in other guises than this? Try as he would, he could not keep the lurid image out of his mind; and sooner or later, he knew, it would have to find its way out, like a splinter of steel from an old wound, in some new allegory.[27]

*The Salem Custom House where Hawthorne found the historical record of Hester Prynne, along with the tattered remains of the letter she was forced to wear.*

The second coincidental event followed soon after. Hawthorne was dismissed from his job when the administration in Washington changed. He was now free to write his story of the scarlet letter, though he worried about supporting his family without a paying job. With the support of his wife and his friends, however, he began writing in the fall of 1849.

## Hawthorne Writes with Intensity

From the time Hawthorne began writing *The Scarlet Letter* in September 1849, he wrote steadily and vigorously until he finished it on February 4, 1850. Arvin says of the intensity with which he wrote that "never before had he been so irresistibly dominated by the creatures of his imagination. The constrained energies of several years had been liberated, and in spite of the storm and stress he had just passed through, he could say that he 'was happier, while straying through the gloom of these sunless fantasies,' than at any time since he had quitted the Old Manse."[28] By January 15,

1850, Hawthorne had finished all but the last three chapters and sent the incomplete manuscript to his publisher, James T. Fields. Fields, pleased with the story, immediately made arrangements to publish it and urged Hawthorne to finish quickly. When he finished the novel, he read the last scene to his wife. Stewart quotes the emotional reactions both of them felt:

> "It broke her heart," Hawthorne wrote to Bridge, "and sent her to bed with a grievous headache, which I look upon as a triumphant success." Of his own reaction on that memorable evening, Hawthorne recalled several years later "my emotions when I read the last scene of the Scarlet Letter to my wife, just after writing it—tried to read it, rather, for my voice swelled and heaved, as if I were tossed up and down on an ocean, as it subsides after a storm."[29]

He sent the completed story to Fields, and on March 16, 1850, *The Scarlet Letter*, which included Hawthorne's essay, "The Custom House," as the introduction, was published.

## Success with the Public and the Critics

*The Scarlet Letter* was an immediate success with the public. The first printing of two thousand copies sold in ten days, and the second printing of three thousand was selling well a month after publication. For Hawthorne, the book earned very little. The book sold for seventy-five cents a copy, and Hawthorne's royalties were 10 percent. Two years later the publisher had sold six thousand copies for a total earning for Hawthorne of $450. Fields reported in July 1852 that fifteen thousand copies of *The Scarlet Letter* had sold in Europe.

The book was also a success with reviewers and leading critics,

*Hawthorne (center) and his publishers.*

who lavished it with praise. Several critics commented on the quality of Hawthorne's description and his humor in the opening essay. Others thought that Hawthorne had captured the Puritan culture well. Several commented on the themes, praising Hawthorne for articulating the feelings of guilt and conveying compassion when he adressed the nature of sin and sorrow. One critic thought Hawthorne compared favorably with the famed British novelist Charles Dickens in his creation of characters and scenes. Hawthorne was satisfied with the reviews and pleased to be recognized as a respected writer.

## *The Scarlet Letter* **Also Draws Objections**

Nevertheless, there were those who objected to *The Scarlet Letter.* Two objections were repeated by sympathetic critics—that the novel had a tone of unrelieved gloom and that it lacked a comic spirit to balance the tragedy of the story. Hawthorne agreed. He told Bridge that *The Scarlet Letter* "is positively a hell-fired story, into which I found it almost impossible to throw any cheering light."[30]

A number of critics objected to the novel on moral grounds. Some called it scandalous. Critic Orestes A. Brownson wrote that public morality is in an unsound state if a novelist goes unpunished for writing a novel about the crime of adultery with "all the charms of a highly polished style."[31]

The citizens of Salem were offended by Hawthorne's introductory essay, "The Custom House," which they felt insulted the town. On March 21, 1850, the Salem *Register* carried this opinion: "Hawthorne seeks to vent his spite . . . by small sneers at Salem, and by vilifying some of his former associates, to a degree of which we should have supposed any gentleman . . . incapable. . . . This chapter has obliterated whatever sympathy was felt for Hawthorne's removal from office."[32]

The belief on the part of Salem's residents that Hawthorne was hostile toward them was well founded. In a letter to Bridge the day after he finished *The Scarlet Letter,* he said that he detested Salem because he thought its citizens were small-minded. After the publication of the book, he acknowledged to Bridge that he had caused the greatest uproar since the persecution of the witches. Hawthorne moved with his family from Salem to Lenox in western Massachusetts in the middle of April, 1850, a month after publication of *The Scarlet Letter.* While in Lenox, Hawthorne's popularity grew to the point that visitors traveled there just to look at the author of *The Scarlet Letter.*

## Hawthorne's Place Among Modern Critics

Since Hawthorne's time, *The Scarlet Letter* has continued to be the object of critical comment. Critics focus on the novel from different perspectives, recognizing that Hawthorne's moral themes are ambiguous; for example, according to the Puritans, Hester's adultery is a sin, but from her perspective, she and Dimmesdale expressed honest feelings for each other. Consequently, it is hardly surprising if critics interpret the themes of *The Scarlet Letter* in a variety of ways. Other modern critics have focused on the form, arguing that the novel is an allegory or a romance or a symbolic novel. Most commentators agree that the novel will outlast all critical interpretations.

*A view of Salem's harbor through Hawthorne's window in the Custom House. Hawthorne left Salem shortly after the publication of* The Scarlet Letter.

# CHAPTER THREE

# The Plot of *The Scarlet Letter*

*T*he *Scarlet Letter* covers a seven-year period during the 1600s in New England, a time when Puritanism was the region's dominant religion. Hawthorne meant for *The Scarlet Letter* to be read as a critique of Puritan attitudes, but at the most basic level, his work functions as a mystery novel. After an introductory essay, in which Hawthorne tells of the circumstances under which he developed the idea for the story, the novel opens by confronting the reader with numerous questions that create an air of mystery. An unmarried mother, Hester Prynne, is being punished for adultery, but she refuses to say who the father of her child is. Other characters soon prove to be keeping secrets of their own. The interactions between the characters as these secrets are gradually unveiled makes up the plot of *The Scarlet Letter*.

## The Custom House

Hawthorne's essay about the Custom House in Salem describes the building, its history, the people who work there, and his thoughts and experiences while he was an employee. Hawthorne reflects on his own ancestors who entered and worked at this port; the most recent ancestors were maritime workers, but the first two generations were Puritan leaders. He feels ashamed of the cruelties these stern individuals inflicted. One slow day at the customhouse, Hawthorne explores the second-floor storage area. He comes upon a scroll with information about a woman named Hester

Prynne and her activities in Massachusetts near the close of the seventeenth century. With the scroll is a tattered letter A, embroidered elaborately with gold thread.

## Chapter 1: The Prison-Door

Hawthorne sets a dark and hostile tone by describing the prison and the gathering crowd of Puritan men and women, all dressed in gray. The prison door is built of dark weathered wood and heavy oak and iron held together with spikes. Heavyset women jeer and call for severe punishment for the wayward woman about to emerge through the prison door. Only one young woman, who urges sympathy, and one blossoming wild rose break up the darkness of the scene, giving the reader reason to speculate on their significance.

## Chapter 2: The Market-Place

Hawthorne enumerates the kinds of inmates that have emerged from the prison door and, in the process, gives the reader a sense of Puritan laws and punishments. Then Hester, wearing an ornately embroidered A on her gray garment, appears clutching her baby in her arms. They are led from the prison to the scaffold in the center of the marketplace. On the balcony of the adjacent meetinghouse sit dignitaries—the governor and his counselors, a judge, a general, and the ministers of the town. Five hundred citizens stare and wait.

## Chapter 3: The Recognition

Coincidentally, a group of Indians accompanied by a white man have happened into town and gather with the Puritans. From the scaffold Hester meets the eyes of the white stranger, who gestures to her to keep quiet. Through the man's questions to the Puritans near him and their answers, the reader learns the background of the event and Hester's punishment—three hours to stand on the platform and for the rest of her life to wear the scarlet A on her breast. The stranger declares that Hester's lover will be revealed. Then the authorities urge Hester to reveal the child's father: first the governor, then the senior minister John Wilson, and finally the junior minister Arthur Dimmesdale, whose urging carries a more sympathetic tone. At each request, Hester refuses. The stranger in the audience adds his request, but still Hester refuses.

After all have failed to make her talk, the Reverend Wilson delivers a one-hour sermon on sin while Hester stands before the crowd holding her baby. At the end of the ordeal, Hester is led back into prison.

## Chapter 4: The Interview

In her cell, Hester is so agitated that jailer Master Brackett describes her as one possessed by Satan and calls in a physician, who turns out to be the white stranger in the crowd. He administers a potion to calm the baby and then one for Hester. The physician is Roger Chillingworth, Hester's husband, who was thought to have been lost at sea. The two acknowledge the wrong they have done to one another, and Chillingworth promises never to harm Hes-

*Hester Prynne stands atop the marketplace scaffold. Dimmesdale stands on the balcony in the background.*

ter or the child. Again he asks her to identify her lover, and again Hester refuses.

## Chapter 5: Hester at Her Needle

Once released from prison, Hester establishes herself in the abandoned thatched cottage granted her by the authorities. In this remote location, Hester has a garden and develops a needlework business, making plain garments for the poor and fancy garments for ceremonial occasions, funerals, and newborns. On trips into town children follow her, shouting cruel insults, and ministers make mini-sermons of her sin for the benefit of small crowds of listeners. Hester is utterly alone but withstands Puritan disapproval in silence.

## Chapter 6: Pearl

Hester's baby grows into a beautiful little girl, whom Hester names Pearl. Hester dresses Pearl, who goes everywhere with her

37

mother in bright-colored garments decorated with elaborate embroidery, a mode of dress deemed inappropriate by Puritans. Pearl responds with silence to local children who speak to her or with shrill shouts if they crowd too close. In her play alone in the woods, her imagination leads her to make puppets of sticks and flowers. From infancy, Pearl focuses not on her mother's face, but on the A. She looks at it, touches it, throws flowers at it. Each of these gestures causes Hester emotional—almost physical—pain. Hester worries about her child, remembering the talk of the townspeople that Pearl might be a demon offspring.

## Chapter 7: The Governor's Hall

One day when Pearl is old enough to run along at her mother's side, Hester goes to Governor Bellingham's mansion to deliver gloves she has embroidered, but, more important, to plead her case for keeping Pearl. Governor Bellingham and many of the townspeople have been promoting a plan to take Pearl from Hester either because, if she is a child of demon origin, she is a stumbling block to Hester's salvation or because, if she is a normal child, she needs a more suitable parent. Hester desperately wants to keep Pearl. Since the governor is presently meeting with the town ministers, Hester must wait. Ignoring all of her mother's requests to be quiet and sit still, Pearl explores the entrance hall and garden outside the window. She studies a suit of armor and calls her mother. Hester looks into the convex mirror of the breastplate and sees a large, exaggerated scarlet letter.

## Chapter 8: The Elf-Child and the Minister

The governor and Mr. Wilson enter followed by Dimmesdale and Chillingworth. Governor Bellingham faces Hester and launches into his argument that Pearl should be taken from her, dressed and disciplined properly, and instructed in Christian truths. In response Hester says that she can teach Pearl what she has learned from being forced to wear the letter—lessons that make her wiser and better. On hearing Hester's claim the governor commands Wilson to examine Pearl in her knowledge of Christian ways. Wilson asks Pearl who made her. Though Pearl knows that the answer is the Heavenly Father, she tells Wilson that she had not been made, but plucked from the rosebush by the prison door. Hester, noting the governor's shock, clutches Pearl and argues defiantly that God has given her the child. She swears that she will die before she allows Pearl to be taken away. She turns to Dimmesdale and pleads with him to speak for her. Nervous, Dimmesdale holds his hand over his heart and argues that the child prevents Hester from worse sin. The governor accepts Dimmesdale's argument and drops the matter, and Hester and Pearl leave. On the way out the governor's sister, Mistress Hibbins, who is reputed to be a witch, calls to Hester to meet her and the Black Man in the forest that night, but Hester declines because she has Pearl to care for.

*Hester vows that she will not allow the governor to take Pearl away from her.*

## Chapter 9: The Leech

Living in disguise, Chillingworth promotes himself as a learned man, and because there is a shortage of people educated in the sciences, he becomes the town doctor. Dimmesdale's congregation observes their minister's declining health and urges Chillingworth to treat him. Chillingworth watches Dimmesdale closely, but after the two arrange to take rooms in a widow's house Chillingworth becomes ever closer, prying into Dimmesdale's soul as well as into his health. Half the townspeople think the arrival of Chillingworth is an arrangement from God; the other half are suspicious of him.

## Chapter 10: The Leech and His Patient

Chillingworth pries into Dimmesdale's thoughts first on one subject and then another. One day while the two men are meeting in a room with a window overlooking the cemetery, Hester and Pearl walk by. Pearl picks burrs and arranges them on Hester's A and throws one at Dimmesdale. She urges her mother to come away from the Black Man because he will get her as he has already gotten Dimmesdale. In the following days, Chillingworth heightens his pressure on Dimmesdale and asks him to speak his thoughts more openly. Dimmesdale refuses to do so. A few days later as Dimmesdale naps soundly in his chair, Chillingworth throws aside the ministerial vestment that always covers Dimmesdale. Chillingworth stares, then turns away, throws up his arms, and stamps his foot. What Chillingworth sees Hawthorne leaves unstated, however.

## Chapter 11: The Interior of a Heart

Chillingworth, informed by whatever he saw on the minister's chest, enters Dimmesdale's inner world with such skill that Dimmesdale is only vaguely uncomfortable in the physician's presence. Dimmesdale becomes weaker and more tortured. The more he conveys his own distress in his sermons to his congregation, the more popular he becomes. Night after night in the dark, Dimmesdale keeps vigil in his room and conjures up visions of his guilt. His torment continues.

## Chapter 12: The Minister's Vigil

*Dimmesdale ascends the scaffold, unnoticed by the passing Reverend Wilson.*

One cloudy May night after midnight when the residents of the town are asleep, Dimmesdale goes to the scaffold where seven years earlier Hester had stood with her child. Dimmesdale shrieks aloud, bringing Governor Bellingham and his sister Mistress Hibbins to their windows, but they do not see him and go back to bed. Reverend Wilson, returning from a visit to the bedside of a dying man, walks by, but he is too preoccupied with the muddy road to notice anyone on the scaffold. Dimmesdale, imagining that he is unable to leave the platform, envisions the whole town discovering him at dawn. Hester, who has been watching at Governor Winthrop's deathbed, arrives on the scene with Pearl and joins Dimmesdale on the scaffold. The three hold hands, and Pearl asks Dimmesdale to stand with her and her mother at noon the next day, but Dimmesdale declines and tells her he will stand with them on judgment day. Dimmesdale asks Hester's help to protect him from Chillingworth. When a meteor passes overhead, lighting up the whole town, Dimmesdale imagines that it is an A outlined in red. Then Chillingworth, who has been ministering to Governor Winthrop, comes by and stops. He reminds Dimmesdale that he needs sleep before he delivers the next day's sermon and takes Dimmesdale home. The next morning Dimmesdale preaches a spectacular sermon. On the way down the pulpit steps the sexton hands him his black glove, which he found on the scaffold. The sexton assumes that Satan has dropped it there and comments that a meteor formed an A for angel at the passing of Governor Winthrop.

## Chapter 13: Another View of Hester
Hester, shocked at seeing Dimmesdale's weakened condition, feels compelled to respond to his request for help against Chillingworth. Hester's seven years of humbly serving the townspeople with her sewing and her attention to the sick have changed their attitude toward her. They show off Hester to strangers as a kind woman who helps the poor and sick. But her suffering and isolation have changed her, taking away the passion and radiance she once had. Hester contemplates the effect Chillingworth is having on Dimmesdale and regrets keeping Chillingworth's true identity secret. She decides to meet with Chillingworth.

## Chapter 14: Hester and the Physician
Hester confronts Chillingworth as he gathers herbs. She observes how Chillingworth's face has changed with fierce, fiendish qualities replacing his former calm and quiet. Hester expresses her regret for keeping Chillingworth's true identity secret and declares her intent to tell Dimmesdale. She asks Chillingworth to forgive the minister and save himself, but he rejects her request and declares that all four lives—mother, daughter, and the two men—are controlled by fate.

## Chapter 15: Hester and Pearl
Hester watches Chillingworth continue his search for plants and expresses her hatred for him, yet she blames herself for marrying

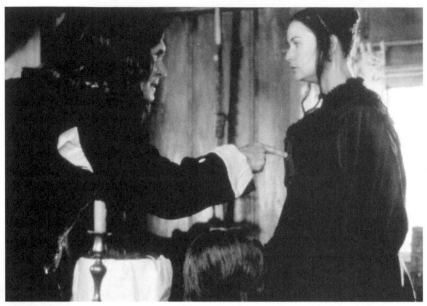

*Chillingworth (left) refuses Hester's request that he forgive Dimmesdale.*

him. Pearl appears with a seaweed shawl decorated with a green A. Hester and Pearl talk about the A and why Hester wears her scarlet letter. Pearl says she knows it is for the same reason that the minister puts his hand over his heart. Hester tries to stop Pearl's questions, but Pearl persists. Finally, Hester firmly says not to tease and threatens to put Pearl in a closet if she asks more questions.

## Chapter 16: A Forest Walk
Determined to warn Dimmesdale of Chillingworth's intentions, Hester takes advantage of an opportunity to meet Dimmesdale on his return from a visit to Indian converts. At the place where her mother has chosen to wait, Pearl wants a story about the Black Man, who, she says, carries a book in which those he meets sign in blood. Pearl wants to know if Hester has ever met him, and Hester tells her that she met him once and that the scarlet letter is his mark. Pearl goes off to play by the brook just when Hester sees the minister approach.

## Chapter 17: The Pastor and His Parishioner
Hester summons Dimmesdale from the path. They greet and review the agony they have suffered over the past seven years be-

fore Hester explains that Dimmesdale's enemy is her husband. Dimmesdale, feeling her accountable, says he cannot forgive her. Unable to bear his disapproving look, Hester draws him to her breast and begs him to forgive her. He realizes that his emotion is sadness, not anger, and forgives her. He says that Chillingworth's revenge is worse than the sin they have committed. Dimmesdale asks Hester for help to get away from Chillingworth. To Hester's suggestion that he escape into the wilderness or to England, Dimmesdale proclaims that he is too weak to go alone. Hester promises that Dimmesdale will not go alone.

## Chapter 18: A Flood of Sunshine

As the two sit on the forest floor making plans to escape to Europe, it is apparent that Hester's isolation and forced exile have made her stronger and freer than she was seven years earlier, while Dimmesdale's personal shame and his popularity within the Puritan community have made him weaker and more ridden with guilt. Both, however, express the joy and determination of the moment. Hester unclasps the A, throws it aside, removes her cap, and lets down her hair, restoring her youth and beauty. At that moment the sun bursts forth from behind clouds. Hester calls Pearl from her play in the forest, but she approaches slowly when she sees the minister.

## Chapter 19: The Child at the Brook-Side

Pearl, standing on the opposite side of the brook, refuses to cross to the mound where her mother and Dimmesdale sit. Throughout Hester's urgings, Pearl points her finger at her mother; when Hester threatens, Pearl stamps her feet and shrieks in a temper tantrum. Only after Hester returns the A to its place on her breast and bundles her hair back under her cap does Pearl cross the stream, satisfied and reassured. When she learns that the minister will not walk into town holding their hands, Hester has to drag her to the minister's side. He kisses her on the forehead, and she runs to the brook and washes the spot.

## Chapter 20: The Minister in a Maze

Dimmesdale has received the honor of delivering the sermon on the occasion of the installation of the new governor, which is known as the election day. On the walk back to town he thinks about his sermon, but finds that the town and its people seem somehow different. Invigorated by his meeting with Hester, he has the impulse to do and say wicked things. Mistress Hibbins stops him and asks if he has been to the woods and made a bargain with the devil, but he says he has only made a bargain for happiness. At home when Chillingworth offers to help him prepare the sermon, Dimmesdale's hand automatically goes to his heart. Dimmesdale refuses and later throws his prepared sermon into the fire and writes a new one.

## Chapter 21: The New England Holiday

In Puritan New England, the installation of a new governor is cause for a public holiday. Hester and Pearl are among the

*Hester and Dimmesdale with Pearl at the brook-side.*

crowd. People, dressed in their Sabbath-day clothes, have left school and work to watch the procession and participate in the games. Livening up the gray throng of Puritans, Indians in feathers and paint and mariners from a ship, the *Spanish Main,* stand among the crowd. A messenger from the ship's captain tells Hester that Chillingworth will also be sailing to England. Chillingworth catches Hester's eye and smiles.

## Chapter 22: The Procession

Hester has no time to collect her thoughts about the captain's news before the procession, featuring bands, military soldiers, and governing dignitaries, begins. At the last is Dimmesdale, who will deliver the election sermon. Hester hopes to catch his eye, but he moves as if unaware of his surroundings. Mistress Hibbins moves close to Hester and refers to Dimmesdale's recent meeting with Hester in the forest; she asks Hester what the minister hides with his hand over his heart. Hester does not answer, and Hibbins gives a loud shriek and leaves. Dimmesdale begins, speaking in rising and falling tones about the human heart filled with sorrow and guilt, seeking sympathy and forgiveness. As he speaks, one of the mariners gives Pearl a message for her mother letting her know that the doctor will bring Dimmesdale aboard the next day.

## Chapter 23: The Revelation

At the close of Dimmesdale's sermon the procession recesses, making its way through the crowd toward the scaffold where Hester stands with Pearl. When Dimmesdale reaches that point he pauses, turns, and calls Hester and Pearl. Chillingworth tries to stop him. Dimmesdale takes Hester and Pearl up the scaffold steps in front of the crowd. He says that he now stands upon the spot where, seven years ago, he should have stood with Hester. He tears the ministerial band away, baring his chest to the horror-stricken crowd and then sinks down. What the crowd sees Hawthorne leaves unstated. Chillingworth bemoans repeatedly that Dimmesdale has escaped him. Near death, Dimmesdale smiles at Pearl and asks for a kiss. Pearl kisses him on the lips, and Dimmesdale and Hester speak their final words to each other. Awestruck, the people look on as their minister dies.

*Dimmesdale bares his chest before the crowd as he confesses his affair with Hester.*

## Chapter 24: Conclusion

What the crowd saw is now revealed. In the days following Dimmesdale's death, those who witnessed the strange event speculate on how the A came to be on Dimmesdale's chest, and some deny that it was even a mark. Nonetheless, Dimmesdale's life and death become a parable that teaches that even saints are sinners. Chillingworth withers away and dies within a year, bequeathing his estate in England and America to Pearl, who eventually becomes the richest woman in New England. Hester and Pearl disappear, and Hester's story grows into a legend. Then one day she returns wearing the A and becomes a confidant whom women seek for advice and consolation. She receives mail and packages from abroad and sews a small child's garment. Pearl, it seems, has married well and has a child of her own. When Hester dies, she is buried in a grave next to Dimmesdale's.

# CHAPTER FOUR

# The Cast of Characters

*T*he Scarlet Letter contains three major adult characters—
Roger Chillingworth, Arthur Dimmesdale, and Hester
Prynne—and the child Pearl, Hester's daughter. Several
minor characters appear from time to time, but they serve to contrast or mirror the major characters or serve as devices to advance
the plot and themes of the story.

## Major Characters

### Roger Chillingworth

When Roger Chillingworth poses as a doctor and enters Hester's
cell, the reader learns that Chillingworth is Hester's husband.
Thought to have been lost at sea, Chillingworth instead had been
captured by Indians. He is much older than Hester and realizes
now that his advanced age and preoccupation with intellectual
studies made him an unsatisfactory husband for the beautiful
young Hester. Although he assures her he will harm neither Hester nor her child, he vows that he will learn who her lover is and
take control of him. Indeed, Chillingworth does identify Dimmesdale as Hester's partner, becomes his doctor and intellectual companion, and eventually takes up residence as a fellow lodger in a
widow's home, an arrangement that allows him to become even
more intimately acquainted with the object of his revenge.

Chillingworth also has a connection with the novel's minor
characters. His scientific knowledge and his knowledge of herbal
medicine learned from the Indians allow him to become the town
doctor. His role as Dimmesdale's doctor and constant companion

*Roger Chillingworth is a symbol of evil in* The Scarlet Letter. *Hawthorne used Chillingworth to develop the theme of revenge, and to create suspense in the novel.*

allows him to be present at state functions and as a consequence he knows Governor Bellingham and senior minister John Wilson. Late in the book he is seen again conversing with the Indian chief and with the captain of the ship docked in the harbor. He is related only indirectly to Governor Bellingham's sister Mistress Hibbins, reputed to be a witch, but they are parallel characters because of the supernatural powers they both apparently possess.

Roger Chillingworth helps drive the plot and develops some of the themes of the novel. First, his relationship to Dimmesdale defines the theme of revenge. Out of malice and a desire for revenge, he chooses to play upon the minister's sense of guilt. In this way, Chillingworth becomes an active participant in Dimmesdale's inner life and helps determine his behavior as well. Second, Chillingworth haunts Hester's world, not necessarily out of malice, but he is still a bothersome presence lurking in the shadows, adding a sneer to every connection between Hester and Dimmesdale. He is at the Governor's house when Hester pleads her case for keeping Pearl. He appears smiling and smirking when Hester meets Dimmesdale at the scaffold. As he collects plants in the field near Hester's cottage, Hester asks him to forgive the minister, but he refuses. He serves to create suspense, making the reader wonder if his identity will come to light and if he will destroy Dimmesdale.

Above all else, for Hawthorne, Chillingworth is a symbol of evil. He hypocritically poses as the doctor, all the while relentlessly working toward Dimmesdale's moral and psychological destruction. Hester's reference to him as the "Black Man that haunts the forest round about us"[33] even more directly links Chillingworth to the epitome of evil, Satan. Hawthorne, through the voice of the narrator, leaves little doubt about Chillingworth's satanic connections by referring to him as a devil. But Dimmesdale escapes Chillingworth's grasp in the end, and the physician is left to wither away and die within a year.

## Arthur Dimmesdale

Arthur Dimmesdale is the town's junior minister, but he regularly preaches Sunday sermons. He is Chillingworth's patient, Hester's secret lover, and Pearl's father. The reader knows from the beginning that Dimmesdale is the minister and learns in chapter nine how closely Dimmesdale associates himself with his physician. Though Hawthorne hints at Dimmesdale's relationship to Hester and Pearl, the reader only learns with certainty the exact nature of these relationships midway through the novel in chapter twelve.

Dimmesdale possesses a sensitive nature and suffers from deteriorating health. Early on, the reader learns that all is not well with Dimmesdale spiritually. At the first scaffold scene when he calls upon Hester to reveal her partner, the narrator says that Dimmesdale seemed frightened and confused and later describes his sallow, troubled face. Ironically, he achieves community popularity that overshadows that of his fellow clergymen because of his spiritual self-doubt and his intellectual talents. The people in Dimmesdale's congregation worry about him and urge Chillingworth to tend his health carefully. Being asked to care for Dimmesdale affords Chillingworth ample opportunity to exact excruciating revenge.

*Arthur Dimmesdale, whose relationship with Hester remains a secret throughout much of the novel, creates an air of mystery and ambiguity in the novel.*

Besides staying close to Chillingworth to receive medical treatment, Dimmesdale finds Chillingworth intellectually stimulating. Dimmesdale takes walks with Chillingworth, and they visit in each other's studies. A man of deep religious faith, Dimmesdale finds Chillingworth's scientific ideas interesting, an outlook unlikely to be found among his colleagues. Thus, Dimmesdale's interest in Chillingworth makes it easier for Chillingworth to gain Dimmesdale's confidence. Dimmesdale clearly has a secret eating away at both his physical and spiritual health. The ambiguity of this secret heightens the suspense in the novel. On one hand the reader wants Dimmesdale to tell the truth, as Chillingworth urges, so that his health will improve. On the other hand the reader is encouraged to be suspicious of Chillingworth even as Dimmesdale is. Even though the reader knows Dimmesdale's secret and Chillingworth's vengeful goal, until Dimmesdale himself is certain of Chillingworth's identity and intent—and that knowledge does not come until chapter seventeen—Dimmesdale appears vulnerable, and the reader feels anxious for him.

Dimmesdale is Hester's lover, but this fact is never stated until chapter seventeen, when Hester meets Dimmesdale in the forest. In the early stages of the novel, Dimmesdale has only a few encounters with Hester, and these are in the context of his ministerial duties. In the first scaffold scene and at the scene in the governor's house, Dimmesdale displays sympathy for Hester, but the reader can attribute his attitude to his kind and sensitive nature.

Dimmesdale has open contact with Hester three times in the novel, and each time he reveals himself as a somewhat weak, self-centered individual. During the midnight scene on the scaffold, he welcomes Hester and holds Pearl's hand, but makes no gesture to acknowledge openly his true relationship with them. Dimmesdale's interpretation of the meteor as a sign meant for him personally is an indication of his self-centeredness. In the forest meeting with Hester, Dimmesdale again reveals self-centeredness and weakness when he holds Hester accountable for keeping Chillingworth's secret until she pleads desperately for his forgiveness. To Hester's suggestions that he escape from Chillingworth, Dimmesdale asks Hester to think and be strong for him because the struggle is too hard for him. Only when Hester promises to escape with him does he have enough nerve to hope.

In the final scene, Dimmesdale's actions are more ambiguous. Some critics assert that he is still self-serving and weak, while others see Dimmesdale as brave for confessing his guilt. He relies on Hester's support as he ascends the scaffold, and he requests a kiss from Pearl before he dies. Dimmesdale escapes in death and leaves his congregation in shock and Hester to care for Pearl alone as she has done since the child's birth. Nonetheless, Dimmesdale does muster the courage to reveal his hypocrisy before the entire town on a day when he has been honored.

Dimmesdale is Pearl's father, but he never fulfills that role; rather he relates to Pearl with nervousness, displayed in his habit of placing his hand over his heart. On the scaffold at midnight and in the forest, when Pearl asks him to join her and her mother, he rejects her and says he will stand with them on judgment day. In the final scene on the scaffold, his death represents the ultimate rejection of his role as husband and father.

In his role as minister, Dimmesdale is a more sympathetic character. He has official dealings with Governor Bellingham and Reverend Wilson, but Dimmesdale is noticeably more sensitive than either of these other two officials. The townspeople venerate him as holy and exemplary, and he fulfills his ministerial duties responsibly. The reader knows him to be remorseful for his sin and

*Dimmesdale dies atop the marketplace scaffold. Dimmesdale's declining health and ultimate demise help convey the theme of suffering and pain associated with hidden guilt.*

pained by the public's adulation for him, although he is never able until the end to tell the truth or take responsibility for his child.

Dimmesdale serves a number of purposes in *The Scarlet Letter.* First, his presence serves to create mystery in the plot. Though Hawthorne provides many clues, the reader is curious through much of the book about the meaning of the gesture of putting his hand on his heart, about the underlying cause of his failing health, and whether or not he ever will face the consequences of his actions. Second, he is important to the other characters in the novel by providing sharp contrasts to their attitudes and behaviors. For example, Hester's sin is public, and she grows stronger; by contrast Dimmesdale's sin is secret, and he grows weaker. Chillingworth is directed and determined in his goal; Dimmesdale, on the other hand, lacks direction and depends on others to provide it. Pearl directly seeks the truth in the questions she asks Dimmesdale; Dimmesdale is hesitant and evasive in response to Pearl and her questions. Third, Dimmesdale's words and actions allow Hawthorne to sharpen his themes with the use of literary devices. Dimmesdale is a symbol of hypocrisy and cowardliness. Hawthorne also uses him to provide profound instances of irony, such as his request on the scaffold that Hester reveal her partner, her pleading with him at the governor's house, and his high standing in the Puritan community despite his sin. Finally, Dimmesdale conveys an important theme—the effect of suffering that results from hidden sin and guilt and how evil works to take advantage of a weak, shame-ridden soul.

## Hester Prynne

Hester Prynne is the main character in *The Scarlet Letter,* the woman who is sentenced to wear the scarlet A for the rest of her life as punishment for adultery. She was born in England and married there. Hawthorne is vague as to how or why Hester came to America, but the reader is told that she is in New England without her husband, who is thought to have been lost at sea. Banished from town as part of her punishment, Hester lives in an abandoned cottage next to the sea and near the forest. She cares for her child and supports herself by sewing for people in the community.

Hester's most constant relationship is with her daughter, Pearl, who brings her mother a complex mixture of pain and pleasure. From infancy, Pearl focuses on her mother's intricately embroidered red A. Every look and every touch from Pearl bring pain to Hester. Innocently, Pearl decorates the letter with flowers and burrs, imitates it with her own green A made of plants, and as she grows older, persists in questioning Hester about the letter's meaning. Hester teaches Pearl as best she can, but since Pearl has no playmates and no opportunity to attend school, Hester worries that Pearl lacks proper training. Hester is sometimes too overwhelmed with her own emotions to discipline her strong-willed daughter and seems helpless to guide or curb Pearl's wild behavior. Yet Hester loves Pearl and needs her to counter the loneliness of her isolated life. Moreover, she takes pride in her beautiful, intelligent, and spirited daughter and dresses her in bright-colored, elaborately embroidered garments, an act of defiance in the stern, gray Puritan community. Mother and daughter are constant companions throughout the course of the story.

Hester is Dimmesdale's lover and remains loyal to him throughout the novel. From the beginning she refuses to reveal his role, even when he asks her to do so, presumably because her revelation would destroy him professionally. For many years they have no direct relationship, only official meetings. When she encounters him alone on the scaffold at midnight, she realizes how much his health has deteriorated due to the actions of Chillingworth. During the meeting between Hester and Dimmesdale in the forest she reveals that she still loves him. By volunteering to escape to England with him, she conveys her longing to share her life with him. She willingly follows him to the scaffold when he calls her to be present during his public revelation. In her final act of loyalty she cradles him in her arms as he dies.

Hester is legally married to Roger Chillingworth. When she was young and naive, he persuaded her to marry him, even though by age and temperament he was a terrible match for a beautiful passionate woman. She obeys Chillingworth's request to keep his identity a secret for many years. When she sees how his revenge is making him an old ugly man and is destroying Dimmesdale, she regrets having remained quiet. Still, she never acts to undermine Chillingworth, although she does declare that she hates him and feels he has wronged her more than she has wronged him.

Hester's most complex relationship is with the townspeople; her posture toward them remains the same throughout the novel. Hester accepts their taunts in silence and comports herself in a

*Hester Prynne's humble and compassionate nature, as well as her courage and strength, illuminate sharp contrasts inherent in numerous themes in the novel.*

humble manner. Inwardly she is resolved to endure their punishment and determined to keep custody of Pearl despite efforts by town leaders to take her daughter away from her. She becomes a town institution, sewing plain garments for the poor and finery for the special occasions of the rich. She lives simply and gives the money she does not need to charity. In this way Hester carves out a role for herself in the community despite her humiliation.

The townspeople's attitude toward Hester changes over time. At first, the poor repay her charity with scorn; the wealthy women for whom she sews act similarly spiteful toward her. Eventually, however, Hester gains the town's trust, and the people come to rely on her helpfulness, her sympathetic nature, and her strength. After Dimmesdale's death Hester travels with Pearl to England but then returns to Salem, where she resumes wearing her gray dress bearing the scarlet A. Then the townspeople, especially the women, elevate her to the role of confidant and counselor, bringing her their problems for her wisdom and their sorrows for her comfort.

Hester has connections to almost all of the minor characters in the novel. Governor Bellingham oversees her punishment and leads a movement to take Pearl from her, forcing Hester to fight for the child's custody. Though he disapproves of her behavior, he employs her to make gloves for him. Master Brackett, the jailer, escorts her from the prison to the scaffold and back to prison, where he brings in Chillingworth to provide medical help. Mistress Hibbins appears to Hester a few times in the story. In each encounter she tries to entice Hester to meet the Black Man in the forest. Senior minister John Wilson is present when Hester is punished on the scaffold and appears at the governor's house when she pleads to keep Pearl, but the two have almost no conversation or interaction. The unnamed captain of the *Spanish Main* brings Hester the news that Chillingworth will sail to England on the same ship on which she and Dimmesdale plan to sail. Most of Hester's encounters with these characters advance the plot, heighten the suspense, or, in the case of Mistress Hibbins, add an element of mystery and the supernatural.

Hester's purpose in the novel is subtle and complex. Interestingly, despite her placement at the center of the plot, she does little to initiate action in the novel. Rather, the plot advances due to action by others who react to her adultery, which took place before the story opens. Through more than half of the novel Hester goes about her simple life of sewing and caring for Pearl. She reacts to Bellingham's plan to take Pearl away and coincidentally finds Dimmesdale on the scaffold in the night, but she initiates neither event. She takes decisive action only twice in the novel—to meet with Chillingworth to announce that she plans to reveal his identity to Dimmesdale and to meet with Dimmesdale to fulfill that plan. Her passivity is necessary in order for Hawthorne to portray the full impact of Puritan laws and values and to illustrate the nature of human cruelty. Because Hester does not react angrily to the inhumane treatment she encounters daily, the reader gains a heightened awareness of the injustice and insensitivity of the townspeople and her own discipline and growing strength.

Finally, through Hester, Hawthorne develops numerous themes that feature contrasting elements. For example, Hester defies society's laws on one occasion, but she complies with those laws consistently for the rest of her life. The reader also sees how guilt publicly acknowledged affects Hester, in sharp contrast to the way Dimmesdale's guilt over his hidden sin affects him. Hester's role also allows for sharp character contrasts—her courage opposed to Dimmesdale's cowardice and her compassion opposed to Chillingworth's revenge. Through Hester, Hawthorne explores the opposing themes of passion and reason: In the beginning Hester is a symbol of passion, while Chillingworth is the epitome of reason. How these traits affect an individual is demonstrated as the characters exchange traits. Reason becomes a greater part of Hester's character and passionate hate overtakes Chillingworth. Finally, through Hester, who had English values instilled in her in her youth, Hawthorne explores the old and the new worlds and the influence of the past on the present. In short, Hester plays a more important role in *The Scarlet Letter* by being who she is than by what she does.

## Pearl

Pearl is the daughter of Hester and Dimmesdale, although he does not acknowledge her publicly as his daughter. She lives in a cottage at the edge of the Puritan community with her mother. Hawthorne portrays her as an intelligent, beautiful, and spirited child and makes much of her wild nature and behavior.

Pearl's wildness can be explained by the circumstances she is in. Other than her mother, she has no relatives or friendly adults to help nurture her. Hester is consumed with earning a living for herself and Pearl and preoccupied with the burden of public shame, her own guilt, and the loneliness of their isolated lives. Because of this isolation Pearl has no playmates and no social outlets such as church or school. When she does enter the town with her mother, in her bright fancy garments, she looks different from the Puritan children, who jeer at her. Often left alone to entertain herself near the forest, Pearl uses her imagination to invent games with nature's elements, her only playmates. Living in these unusual circumstances she develops into an unruly, strong-willed child.

Hawthorne, however, clearly intended that the reader also see Pearl as a symbol. Most notably she is a manifestation of Hester's psyche. In the early years when Hester's inner turmoil is most pronounced, Pearl's behavior reflects it—flitting from frowns and clenched fists to laughter to rage to sobbing out her

*Hester stands before the town governors to receive her punishment.*

love for her mother. When Pearl is old enough to run along at her mother's side, the Puritan children tease and taunt, and Pearl responds with anger and rage. The narrator refers to her as a manifestation of the scarlet letter. In appearance and action Pearl is a symbol of the scarlet letter and all the turmoil that it represents to Hester.

Hawthorne also gives Pearl other symbolic roles. He associates her with nature and describes the sympathy she has with the birds and animals. She decorates her hair and body with wild flowers and makes puppets of sticks and weeds. The narrator suggests that she has a kinship with the wildness in nature. To the Puritan mind nature means wildness, and wildness means untamed passion, and, therefore, sin. Thus, it is no surprise to Hester that some folks in town think Pearl a demon child. Moreover, Hawthorne creates Pearl as a symbol of truth. Pearl asks both Dimmesdale and Hester if Dimmesdale will stand beside her and her mother and take their hands. She rejects him until the end when he does stand with them. Her rejection suggests that she knows he is false. Likewise she rejects Chillingworth. Again with a child's intuition, she senses that Chillingworth is bad, like the Black Man in the forest. Because Hawthorne has created Pearl with mysterious qualities and described her with numerous nature metaphors, she maintains an ambiguity that elicits a variety of interpretations.

## Minor Characters

### Governor Bellingham

Governor Bellingham, the leader of the Massachusetts settlement and stern keeper of Puritan law, presides at civil functions. He appears several times in the novel and temporarily raises suspense when he tries to take Pearl from Hester and when he appears in the window in response to Dimmesdale's midnight shriek. He makes his final appearance in the procession on election day.

### Master Brackett

Master Brackett is the jailer who takes Hester from prison in the opening scene to the scaffold for her punishment. He returns her to her cell and calls in Chillingworth to minister to her health.

### Mistress Hibbins

Mistress Hibbins is Governor Bellingham's sister. She appears to have supernatural powers. More than once, she asks Hester to join her with the Black Man.

*Hester and Pearl shy away under the gaze of Chillingworth.*

# John Wilson

John Wilson is the senior clergyman in Boston, the minister who delivers the hour-long sermon on sin as Hester stands on the scaffold holding her baby.

# The Puritan Townspeople

Hawthorne treats the Puritan townspeople as a unified hostile group, except for an occasional young woman with a tender heart. He shows that with time they grow tolerant and finally sympathetic and loving toward Hester.

# Unnamed Indian Chief

Indians make two appearances in the book—when Hester is punished on the scaffold and on election day.

*Mistress Hibbins contemplates the accusation that she is a witch.*

# Unnamed Captain of the *Spanish Main*

The captain of the *Spanish Main* appears with his mariners at the election day celebration. Like the Indians, the mariners stand apart as symbols of the wilderness in contrast to the Puritans, who represent the restrictions of civilized society.

# CHAPTER FIVE

# Literary Analysis

C ritics have identified many significant themes in *The Scarlet Letter,* and the book is rich enough in symbol and imagery to justify many interpretations.

## The Consequences of Defying Society's Rules

Literary critic Claudia Durst Johnson contends that *The Scarlet Letter* is really about the consequences of breaking the moral code, in this case a moral law. Because Puritan society in America during the 1600s was moralistic, rigid, stern, cold, and punitive, it demanded that violation of its rules be severely punished. In a moment of passion Hester and Dimmesdale break the law against adultery. When her baby is born, the Puritan authorities punish Hester according to the law, and she emerges from prison with a scarlet A sewn on the front of her garment. For Hester, the consequences are immediate and public as she is taunted by the authorities and the Puritan crowd for three hours. However, because Hester refuses to reveal her partner, Dimmesdale escapes immediate punishment. All the characters experience the consequences of their defiance throughout the entire seven years covered by the story, as Hester, Dimmesdale, and Pearl interact with each other and the rest of the story's characters.

Hester suffers continual humiliation and isolation. The rich and the poor stare at the A, her badge of sin. Chillingworth touches it, and Pearl naively outlines it with burrs picked in the cemetery, each a humiliating reminder of her transgression. Hester's humiliation is matched by the loneliness of isolation. She is banished from the village to live in a cottage at the edge of the wilderness. Whenever she enters the community a vacant circle forms around her into which no Puritan enters to touch her or speak with her. She is never without a reminder of the consequences of violating society's rules.

Dimmesdale suffers in private the consequences of defying society's rules. Hester, who thinks he is luckier because he does not have to endure daily public humiliation, is unaware how severely he is suffering until she encounters him at his midnight vigil and sees how weak and emaciated he has become. Because Dimmesdale's transgression is unknown and unsuspected by the Puritan community, he suffers further from knowing he is a hypocrite. Out of this private suffering he delivers heartfelt sermons, which the Puritan community finds particularly moving. Their approval only makes his life more tortured, and he develops the nervous habit of holding his hand over his heart whenever he is reminded of Hester or Pearl. In his conversation with Hester in the wood he reveals that long ago he should have made public his own guilt. What appears at first to be Dimmesdale's luck in escaping the fate that Hester suffers turns out to have caused him insufferable pain. Even though Hester suggests that he escape with her to England, he knows he cannot. Finally, he confesses his guilt publicly and then dies, the only escape he sees for his seven-year hypocrisy.

Pearl does not break society's rules, but she suffers the consequences because she is the manifestation of Hester and Dimmesdale's defiance of those rules. She has no friends or playmates. She cannot go to school with other children; instead she learns to create a world of imaginary friends out of the plants and animals of the forest. In their isolated circumstances Hester cannot muster the strength and clarity of vision to guide Pearl in her upbringing, and Pearl develops

*Hester Prynne endures humiliation and isolation throughout the novel.*

61

a wild and willful nature as a result. Even though she is an innocent bystander, she still experiences the consequences of her parents' transgression. Moreover, Pearl is a clear allusion to the biblical parable of a man who purchases a pearl of great price, and indeed, Pearl's mother—and ultimately her father—do pay a great price.

## The Psychological Effect of Sin

The psychological effect of sin on an individual is another theme. Sin affects a character's mind, heart, and spirit in accordance with that person's own concept of sin, or moral right and wrong. The way each major character sees sin may or may not differ from society's view. In an essay, "Sin, Isolation, and Reunion—Form and Content in *The Scarlet Letter*," critic John C. Gerber says, "There is, for example, no such thing as uniformity in the concept of sin. To assume this is to confuse the characters and to misinterpret most of the important speeches. Sin in *The Scarlet Letter* is a violation of only that which the sinner *thinks* he violates. . . . To speak, therefore, even of adultery or hypocrisy without discovering what they mean to each individual is to become hopelessly confused about what Hawthorne is doing."[34] Moreover, the characters' personality traits also affect the way they respond to their perceived sins. For the reader this means that Hawthorne provides no simple standard for assessing sin.

Though Hester is being punished for adultery, she does not feel pangs of guilt over her transgression. She does not feel that she sinned against God or nature. She is a genuinely affectionate and passionate person, and she acted in accordance with those qualities. In the forest scene, she agrees when Dimmesdale says that they never violated the sanctity of a human heart—a worse transgression, in his view. Hester also feels that she has not done anything for which she deserves punishment. Although she acts with humility and remains silent in the face of insults, she stands by her beliefs, in effect thumbing her nose at Puritan society by decorating her scarlet letter with elaborate gold embroidery and by dressing Pearl in bright and fancy clothes, which contrast with the dull uniformity of the Puritan community.

Hester's remorse takes two forms. First, she regrets upsetting the community's order by breaking an important rule. Gerber explains, "Not conscious of being a sinner in the orthodox sense of the word, she is nevertheless bitterly aware of the fact that she and Dimmesdale have introduced an act of disorder into an orderly universe."[35] Hester's regret manifests itself in her worry about Pearl's hostile behavior toward the Puritan children— her shrieking and attacking them with stones—and her erratic behavior at home. Hester believes it is somehow related to her own transgression. Her worry brings her to tears, and sometimes she feels assured only when the child sleeps. Hester loves Pearl and is filled with remorse at the thought that her adultery upset order and somehow produced a distorted, damaged child.

*Hester and Dimmesdale embrace passionately.*

Hester also feels remorse over her agreement not to reveal Chillingworth's identity. Keeping this secret violates her own nature and harms Dimmesdale. By keeping Chillingworth's secret she has sinned against her own natural affection and her belief in the virtue of truth. Moreover, her silence gives Chillingworth the opportunity to work his revenge on Dimmesdale. Hester tries to redeem herself by pleading with Chillingworth to abandon his scheme of revenge and by informing Dimmesdale of Chillingworth's identity.

Hester is spared the psychological destruction of guilt, however, because she defines her own sins and acts to make amends. Her courage and quiet determination counter Puritan anger until she gradually gains the community's respect and ultimately their admiration.

Dimmesdale's perception of his own sin is closer to the Puritan community's beliefs than Hester's perception of her transgression is. Until his conversation with Hester in the forest, however, the reader cannot be certain if he is simply an impure mortal like the

*Hester was banished from Puritan society as part of her punishment for adultery.*

other townspeople or if he is both an adulterer and hypocrite. The latter turns out to be the case. Gerber explains:

> To refrain from confessing his adultery is to add sin against the community to sin against God. The issue, in fact, is more than raised; it is forced home. In view of the entire town he is compelled by the Reverend Mr. Wilson to exhort Hester to reveal the identity of the baby's father. Thus, before the whole community, by failing to confess his guilt Dimmesdale breaks the community's cardinal precept.[36]

Dimmesdale's concept of his own sin makes him feel guilty, and his psychological makeup prevents him from coping with either his sin or guilt. Dimmesdale is a sensitive, self-absorbed man, educated in England, now ministering to a strict and punitive wilderness community. Because he is the youngest minister in the town and has much to lose, he chooses to protect his reputation rather than to stand with Hester on the scaffold at the beginning of the novel. When he later tries to confess his sin from the pulpit, he talks in generalities, leading the congregation to admire him as a genuinely humble man. This undeserved adulation, ironically, only tortures Dimmesdale further.

Dimmesdale's psychological suffering is compounded because he knows he is weak and cowardly. Dimmesdale is uncomfortable with Chillingworth and suspicious of him, but he does nothing to get away from him and continues to deteriorate under Chillingworth's malicious influence. Dimmesdale declines in health and spirit throughout the story until the magnitude of his guilt and shame overcomes him.

Chillingworth is guilty of three sins, although for the most part he does not see his behavior as sinful. The first is the wrong done to Hester by persuading her to marry him, a sin to which he admits. His second sin is to ignore Hester, conceal his identity, and deceive the Puritan community by identifying himself as a learned doctor. Chillingworth does not see this deception as sinful, but as a means to achieve his objective. This objective—to find Hester's lover and take revenge—is his third sin. Chillingworth expresses no remorse in pursuing this sinful goal. Accustomed to the mental discipline of a scholar, Chillingworth pursues Dimmesdale's destruction in the same methodical, rational manner he would use to study a scientific topic. Every time he has an opportunity to sting

*Chillingworth, shown here with Hester, posed as a learned doctor, concealing his true identity from the townspeople.*

Dimmesdale's conscience, he expresses glee. Sin is not on his mind, and remorse, guilt, and shame are not part of his psyche.

In fact, Chillingworth feeds on his search for revenge. Once Dimmesdale escapes from him by dying, Chillingworth also withers and dies within a year. Still, as warped as Chillingworth is, he leaves his entire estate to Pearl. Chillingworth's sin turns him into a diabolical creature, but this final action hints at the possibility of redemption for even the worst sinner.

## Symbolism in *The Scarlet Letter*

Hawthorne's craftsmanship in *The Scarlet Letter* invites the reader to use imagination to perceive multiple levels of meaning in the text. Hawthorne saw life as complex and wanted his readers to think more deeply about the novel and not settle on a single, definitive interpretation. One of the author's most skillful strategies is his use of symbols, which gives the novel layers of meaning and affords the reader the chance to view events in the plot from various perspectives. Some of the more prominent symbols are the A, Pearl, and mirrors.

The most obvious symbol is the scarlet letter itself. Its most obvious meaning is adultery. As such, Hester's A provides Chillingworth with an excuse to abandon her and to search out her lover and take revenge on him. Hester's A makes Dimmesdale nervous every time he sees it because it reminds him of his own status as an adulterer. Hawthorne means for the letter to be seen in other ways as well. For example, the Puritan officials and the citizens are proud of having properly upheld the law and punished sin, and the A becomes a symbol of their pride. In contrast to the Puritans' drab simplicity, Hester embroiders the letter elaborately, making its very fanciness a small symbol of defiance. By contrast the letter is a symbol of order for Pearl, who sees the A on her mother's breast and finds reassurance in it. When she sees her mother in the forest without it, she refuses to come near until Hester has returned the letter to its usual place.

Hawthorne encourages the reader to think more deeply about the letter's symbolism by suggesting that the A has meanings other than adultery. For example, during Dimmesdale's night vigil a meteor appears, and he sees it as an A meant for him. The next day when returning the glove Dimmesdale dropped on the scaffold, the sexton marvels at the great letter A, which he interprets to stand for Angel, signifying Governor Winthrop's death. As Hester wins the confidence of the community and she is called upon to tend the sick, many people say the A means Able because she is a powerful and sympathetic caregiver.

In any case, the A is clearly associated with inner guilt. Hawthorne refers twice to the mark on the minister's body, suggesting that an A has appeared on Dimmesdale's chest in the place where he puts his hand, though Hawthorne never states that it is definitely visible. After the revelation most people say they saw an A: Some think that Dimmesdale inflicted the torture on himself, some think Chillingworth used drugs and magic to make it appear, and some think the tooth of remorse gnawed its way out from Dimmesdale's heart. The reader, however, is left with plenty of latitude in interpreting the scarlet A.

Closely associated with the A is Pearl; she is, after all, the embodiment of the actions that led to Hester's having to wear the scarlet letter. In an 1886 article in the *Atlantic Monthly*, Hawthorne's son Julian writes, "Pearl, as we are frequently reminded, is the scarlet letter made alive, capable of being loved,

*The letter A on Dimmesdale's chest symbolizes his inner guilt.*

and so endowed with a manifold power of retribution for sin. The principle of her being is the freedom of a broken law."[37] Hawthorne refers to her as a flower of passion and freedom. As such, Pearl's defiance and disobedience represent the undisciplined nature of passion ungoverned by reason. Both Hester's red A and Pearl are reminders of adultery, manifestations of passion and the disorder of undisciplined nature.

Pearl also symbolizes nature, which, in the Puritan mind, is something to be controlled and overcome. In an essay titled "Pearl and the Puritans," critic Chester E. Eisinger says, "According to Puritan theory, adherence of the unregenerate man to nature and natural law will lead to a life of riot and confusion. Such a man is a creature of instincts, carrying his appetites and ambitions to excess. No one can doubt, says [Puritan religious leader] John Cotton, 'the depravation of nature.'"[38] Hawthorne repeatedly compares Pearl to various natural elements: a bird, a butterfly, a flake of sea-foam, a diamond, and a brook. Her very name overtly invites comparison to a natural object. Moreover, Pearl is at home in nature. On one occasion, Pearl entertains herself making boats of birch bark, picking up a jellyfish, tossing white foam and catching it, and making a garment of seaweed that she decorates with a green A. Pearl is so closely identified with nature that the narrator says that the forest tries to be her playmate; it offers her partridgeberries, and the creatures—the partridge, the pigeon, the squirrel, and the fox—hardly move when she comes near.

As a creature of nature, Pearl symbolizes the qualities of disorder, instinct, and excess. She is defiant, she runs wild, flitting like a sprite or an elf. Her instincts allow her to sense a connection to Dimmesdale and to understand the nature of Chillingworth's ill will toward the minister. She is excessive in her unrelenting focus on Hester's A.

Another symbol is the mirror, which in the novel can take a number of forms. Critic Richard Chase says, "Inevitably Hawthorne's symbol for the imagination was the mirror. . . . In the introduction to *The Scarlet Letter,* for example, he uses the mirror to suggest that which gives frame, depth, and otherness to reality. His fictions are mirror-like."[39] In *The Scarlet Letter,* mirrors provide those who look in them with unrealistic pictures, either distorted or more perfect than the actual object. On a deeper

*Pearl plays with seashells on the earthen floor of the cottage where she and Hester live. Pearl symbolizes nature and freedom in* The Scarlet Letter.

level of interpretation, these reflections highlight the strange and isolated lives of Hester and Pearl and the difficulty involved in seeing reality clearly. For example, once, when Pearl is an infant, Hester sees herself reflected in Pearl's eyes, but the image she sees is a fiend. When Hester and Pearl see themselves reflected in the polished armor in the governor's house, they see other distorted images. The convex shape of the breastplate reflects the scarlet letter in magnified proportions, and the headpiece of the armor distorts Pearl's face into an implike creature. By using distorted reflections, Hawthorne implies that the perception of reality, in mirrors as in life, can be distorted by the circumstances.

Hawthorne uses mirror images of Pearl in water to symbolize the meaning of the moment or to reinforce an idea. In one instance Pearl plays alone and sees her own image. She thinks it is a little maid, who invites her to come into the pool. When Pearl steps in she recognizes the reality of her own feet. The scene reinforces Hawthorne's message that Pearl's life is isolated and that she lacks contact with other children. In the scene with Hester and Dimmesdale in the forest, they see Pearl reflected in a pool as she refuses to cross the brook. Pearl, adorned with flowers and foliage, stands in sunlight, and the smooth quiet pool reflects a perfect image. The perfect image of Pearl parallels the perfect moment that Hester and Dimmesdale have found together in the forest, but neither the image of Pearl nor her parents' moment can last because neither is real. Throughout the book Hawthorne uses the symbol of reflections, which never conform to reality, to reinforce a distortion in the circumstances of the characters.

## Imagery in *The Scarlet Letter*

Hawthorne uses color and shades of light and dark to set the tone of the novel, but he also uses them to reinforce meaning. However, what a color means often changes in the novel. *The Scarlet Letter* contains over four hundred images involving light and color, and their meanings come from the context in which they appear. The most prominent images are shades of red and black, sunlight and darkness.

Red, for example, represents brightness and beauty in some situations, and in others it represents sin. The roses by the prison and in Governor Bellingham's garden suggest beauty and life as do the rosy cheeks of the young woman in the crowd who sympathizes with Hester. On the other hand, the A is red and its direct connection to Hester's adultery is suggestive of sin. The Indians wear red finery, creating an association with their supposed wildness and recklessness. The red glow said to emit from Chillingworth's eyes suggests the devil.

Sunlight has the same warm implications as many of the red images. When it appears—and its appearance in the novel is rare—it suggests health, love, or revelation of truth. For example, the sun shines on Hester and Dimmesdale in the forest only temporarily when they express their love and true feelings; Dimmesdale's revelation of truth at the end occurs in full sunlight.

Black, as well as shades of gray, is as prominent as red. Primarily, gray is used to suggest gloom, a preoccupation with reason, and a lack of imagination, passion, or compassion. For example, the gray-clad Puritans follow the law with rigid reason and show no compassion for Hester. Darkness and gray are also closely identified with evil, secrecy, and falsehood. The chapter on Dimmesdale, "The Interior of a Heart," in which Dimmesdale's guilt is portrayed, contains over twenty images in gray. The situations in which black appears are more ambiguous. The forest is dark and wild, home to the mysterious Black Man, yet Pearl is at home in the forest and finds items there that stimulate her imagination. Although black is synonymous with evil and is often associated with the devil, as in the references to the Black Man and to Chillingworth, Hester and Pearl have black, beautiful hair, and Pearl and the Indians have striking black eyes. The appropriate interpretation of images in black, like those in red, depend on the context and may range from beauty to evil.

## Ambiguity in *The Scarlet Letter*

Critics have repeatedly commented on Hawthorne's reliance on ambiguity in *The Scarlet Letter*. Critic Hyatt H. Waggoner says that "it is not surprising that the so-called ambiguity device should be one of the most characteristic features of his [Hawthorne's] writing and that

*Dimmesdale appears here dressed in a black overcoat. The symbolic function of black varies in the novel, depending on context.*

a more generalized ambiguity should be so typical of it."[40] In particular, two recurring themes, the contrast between the Old World and the New World, and the head versus heart distinction, are fraught with ambiguity.

The Puritan community was settled by people attempting to escape the Old World and begin anew. Yet some who settle in the New World remember their past while others have lost sight of it. Hawthorne represents England as a society of joy and merriment, one that accepts nature and what is natural, a place of elegance and nobility. New England he portrays as somber and stern, a society that rejects nature as an evil wilderness to be dominated, a society that builds functional structures. These opposite worlds are manifested in Hawthorne's depictions of community events, Bellingham's house, Chillingworth, Pearl, and Hester. Through most of the novel, the reader could rightly assume that Hawthorne prefers the Old World and its idealized image of the past over the new Puritan community, but Hester's return to New England at the end of the novel casts doubt on this assumption.

Most of Hawthorne's descriptions of the Puritan public relate to the New World. Yet, in the opening scene as Hester stands before the Puritan crowd to receive her punishment, memories flash before her mind of her Old World village, her parents, and London houses and cathedrals. Her memory of the Old World offers only brief respite from the present reality. The prison is dark, surrounded by burdocks; on the scaffold to which she is led stands a pillory for punishment of sinners. In the crowd heavy women in dull frocks call each other gossips. Had they been in charge of punishment they would have branded Hester on her forehead. Black-robed ministers condemn her from the balcony above. At the beginning, Hawthorne paints a joyless picture of the New World in contrast to the picture of the Old World in Hester's memory.

Near the end of the novel the New Englanders celebrate a public holiday called Election Day. Hawthorne contrasts the events that occurred in Old England for such occasions, which were celebrated with bonfires, banquets, pageantries, and processions. The New England event is dull and joyless by comparison. Yet Hawthorne also says that the first generations of New World inhabitants brought the darkest attitudes of Puritanism with them to America, which their descendants have not shed, suggesting that the Old World was by no means perfect.

Governor Bellingham and Roger Chillingworth both represent a blend of the New and Old Worlds. In New World style, Bellingham condemns Hester and leads the effort to take Pearl from her care and place the child in a proper Puritan home. However, the governor lives in a mansion reminiscent of Old England. A uniformed serving-man greets guests at the door, and visitors are led into a long, oak-paneled hall that is lined with portraits. It is furnished with Elizabethan furniture and heirlooms from Bellingham's paternal English home. The governor has an English flower garden, but in it grow New World cabbages and pumpkins. Clearly, the governor retains more of the Old World than do most of the citizens he governs. Chillingworth also represents both worlds. Educated in England, he represents the scholarly training of English universities, but having lived with Indian tribes, he also represents knowledge of nature. Despite his own adaptation to the New World, in the end, by willing his estate to Pearl, Chillingworth makes it possible for her to return to the Old World.

Pearl is the only major character in the novel to have been born in the New World, yet she is associated only with Old World images. Her appearance is elegant and colorful. Playful and imaginative, she resembles none of the rigid Puritan children. To her, nature is home, and nature welcomes her. At the end of the novel, Hester takes Pearl to England where she grows up, marries a nobleman, bears a child, and makes a new life.

Hester is Old World in style and values. She is beautiful, sensual, passionate, and natural. She exhibits her luxuriant Renaissance-style artistry in the embroidery of her A and in Pearl's garments. The stern punitive ways of Puritan women are foreign to her. In the forest meeting with Dimmesdale she longs to reignite her relationship with him and escape to Europe. After Dimmesdale dies, she takes Pearl to England and stays until Pearl is a young woman.

Hester returns to New England of her own free will, however, because it is the place where she committed her sin and experienced her sorrow. Hester has, in fact, become an American. She takes up her task of helping others and becomes the comforting counselor that women seek in time of trouble. Still, after she dies, her grave is marked with a slab of slate engraved with a shield and words implying Old World heraldry: "ON A FIELD, SABLE, THE LETTER A, GULES [is made red]."[41]

Hawthorne's own stance regarding the values of the Old and New Worlds is ambiguous, even though he seems to prefer Old World values. Humans often glorify the past from the perspective of a later time, yet the hope of returning to that past is unrealistic, as Dimmesdale's decision not to escape to England and Hester's return to New England suggest. However preferable one's memories may be, one's relationship to the present society becomes ingrained, and its sheer familiarity has a compelling attraction. Only Pearl, because she is a child, is isolated enough from Puritan society to leave it behind. Finally, which world is better seems unimportant; what is important is what rings true for the individual.

Hawthorne also explores another set of opposing concepts—those symbolized by the head and the heart. The head signifies thought, reason, and morality grounded in theology. The heart signifies passion, emotion, and nature as a moral guide. Critic Donald A. Ringe explains, "The head and the heart may be called respectively thought and emotion, or perhaps reason and passion. To a certain extent, the heart may be equated with nature and the head with art, that is, intellectual activity in philosophy, art, or science. . . . We must not assume that Hawthorne placed his entire faith in either head or heart; rather, both are necessary elements that must be present in every man. Nor can we assume that either is inherently good or bad."[42] Hawthorne seems through much of the novel to prefer the qualities of passion that Hester represents, but a closer analysis indicates that he is interested in how characters with traits of passion and intellect survive in the Puritan society. "The Puritan society is an evil one—a society which collectively has committed the sins of Ego and Pride. . . . In this society, Hawthorne places three characters who represent three of several possibilities for action in the evil world."[43]

For all of his intellect and knowledge and his moral philosophy based on theology and reason, Dimmesdale is predominantly a character of heart and emotion. For example, in his forest conversation with Hester, he reminds her that they never violated the sanctity of the heart, suggesting that he favors emotion over reason. His preaching is emotional and inspiring. When he has to choose between heart and reason, however, he is unable to follow his heart and escape with Hester. On the scaffold his words reveal that finally he follows the supernatural system that his reasoning and training have helped him construct.

In contrast to other characters, Chillingworth carries the concept of the head to the extreme. He is the scientific experimenter concocting potions for Dimmesdale and other patients. He is a master strategist who plots Dimmesdale's destruction. Critic Richard Chase says, "Chillingworth unites intellect with will and coldly and with sinister motives analyzes Dimmesdale. This is the truly diabolic act in Hawthorne's opinion. It is what he calls the Unpardonable Sin and it is worse than the sins of passion."[44] Yet, according to Hawthorne, Chillingworth's character is not quite unambiguously evil; in the end he acts generously by leaving his fortune to Hester's child.

Hester, at the beginning of the novel, represents the heart. She is passionate, emotional in her hysteria after the ordeal on the scaffold, and simply honest. She determines what is moral by what is natural. However, circumstances force her to move toward thought and reason. She must figure out how to live in her

*Hester's passion is symbolically confined beneath her gray cap and dress.*

isolation and survive Puritan cruelties. She has a duty to rear Pearl and must think about the best ways to earn a living. Chase says, "When she puts on her gray cap and becomes a kind of social worker, her color and passion, her indeterminate, instinctual being is curbed and controlled."[45] With difficulty, Hester learns to use her mind to survive and to care for Pearl. In the end she returns to New England.

Hawthorne expresses no clear preference for head or heart, but seems to indicate that human beings are blends of the two in varying proportions. The proportion in which head and heart are present is unimportant; its value can best be measured by the way individuals with these qualities function in the reality of their environment.

# Notes

## Introduction: America's First Great Novelist

1. Sculley Bradley, Richmond Croom Beatty, and E. Hudson Long, *The American Tradition in Literature*, 3rd ed., vol. 1. New York: W.W. Norton, 1967, p. 596.
2. Bradley et al, *The American Tradition in Literature*, p. 596.
3. Randall Stewart and Dorothy Bethurum, eds., *Classic American Fiction: Edgar Allan Poe, Nathaniel Hawthorne, Herman Melville, Henry James*. Chicago: Scott, Foresman, 1954, p. 55.
4. Quoted in Nathaniel Hawthorne, *The Scarlet Letter*. New York: Washington Square Press, 1994, p. 291.
5. Quoted in Seymour L. Gross, ed., *A Scarlet Letter Handbook*. San Francisco: Wadsworth, 1960, p. 125.
6. Richard Harter Fogle, *Hawthorne's Fiction: The Light and the Dark*. Norman: University of Oklahoma Press, 1964, p. 139.
7. Alison Easton, *The Making of the Hawthorne Subject*. Columbia: University of Missouri Press, 1996, p. 197.

## Chapter 1: The Life of Nathaniel Hawthorne

8. Gloria C. Erlich, *Family Themes and Hawthorne's Fiction: The Tenacious Web*. New Brunswick, NJ: Rutgers University Press, 1984, p. 49.
9. Randall Stewart, *Nathaniel Hawthorne: A Biography*. New Haven, CT: Yale University Press, 1948, p. 5.
10. Quoted in Stewart, *Nathaniel Hawthorne: A Biography*, p. 11.
11. Newton Arvin, *Hawthorne*. New York: Russell & Russell, 1961, p. 22.
12. Arlin Turner, *Nathaniel Hawthorne: A Biography*. New York: Oxford University Press, 1980, p. 53.
13. Stewart, *Nathaniel Hawthorne: A Biography*, p. 44.
14. Quoted in Arvin, *Hawthorne*, pp. 88–89.
15. Erlich, *Family Themes and Hawthorne's Fiction*, p. 101.
16. Newton Arvin, ed., *The Heart of Hawthorne's Journals*. Boston: Houghton Mifflin, 1929, p. 133.
17. Hawthorne, *The Scarlet Letter*, p. 31.

18. Arvin, *Hawthorne*, p. 164.

19. Turner, *Nathaniel Hawthorne: A Biography,* p. 233.

20. Turner, *Nathaniel Hawthorne: A Biography,* p. 242.

21. Arvin, *Hawthorne*, p. 230.

## Chapter 2: Historical Background for *The Scarlet Letter*

22. Norman Foerster, ed., *American Prose and Poetry,* 3rd ed. Boston: Houghton Mifflin, 1947, p. 6.

23. Hawthorne, *The Scarlet Letter*, p. x.

24. Arvin, ed., *The Heart of Hawthorne's Journals,* p. 16.

25. Alfred S. Reid, *The Yellow Ruff &* The Scarlet Letter: *A Source of Hawthorne's Novel.* Gainsville: University of Florida Press, 1955, p. 118.

26. Turner, *Nathaniel Hawthorne: A Biography,* p. 228.

27. Arvin, *Hawthorne*, pp. 152–53.

28. Arvin, *Hawthorne*, p. 157.

29. Stewart, *Nathaniel Hawthorne: A Biography,* p. 95.

30. Quoted in Stewart, *Nathaniel Hawthorne: A Biography,* p. 97.

31. Quoted in Stewart, *Nathaniel Hawthorne: A Biography,* p. 97.

32. Quoted in Stewart, *Nathaniel Hawthorne: A Biography,* p. 98.

## Chapter 4: The Cast of Characters

33. Hawthorne, *The Scarlet Letter*, p. 77.

## Chapter 5: Literary Analysis

34. John C. Gerber, *Twentieth Century Interpretations of* The Scarlet Letter: *A Collection of Critical Essays.* Englewood Cliffs, NJ: Prentice-Hall, 1968, p. 105.

35. Gerber, *Twentieth Century Interpretations of* The Scarlet Letter, p. 108.

36. Gerber, *Twentieth Century Interpretations of* The Scarlet Letter, p. 110.

37. Quoted in Gross, *A Scarlet Letter Handbook,* San Francisco: Wadsworth, 1960, p. 82.

38. Quoted in Gross, *A Scarlet Letter Handbook,* p. 85.

39. Richard Chase, *The American Novel and Its Tradition.* Garden

City, NY: Doubleday, 1957, pp. 70–71.

40. Quoted in Gerber, *Twentieth Century Interpretations of* The Scarlet Letter, p. 67.

41. Hawthorne, *The Scarlet Letter,* p. 276.

42. Quoted in Gerber, *Twentieth Century Interpretations of* The Scarlet Letter, p. 68.

43. Quoted in Gerber, *Twentieth Century Interpretations of* The Scarlet Letter, p. 69.

44. Chase, *The American Novel and Its Tradition,* p. 78.

45. Chase, *The American Novel and Its Tradition,* p. 77.

# For Further Exploration

1. *The Scarlet Letter* has been called a historical novel. Identify examples that portray the laws, dress, inhabitants, and setting of the New England Puritan community. What does Hawthorne reveal in his language about his attitude toward this community? *See also* Perry Miller, *The New England Mind: The Seventeenth Century.* Cambridge, MA: Harvard University Press, 1953, and Alison Easton, *The Making of the Hawthorne Subject.* Columbia: University of Missouri Press, 1996.

2. *The Scarlet Letter* has been called a tragedy—a story with a tragic hero, who sometimes has a fatal flaw; an inevitable force that works against the hero; and a struggle leading to the outcome. Which character or characters fit the definition of tragic hero? Identify the elements of tragedy that apply. *See also* Hyatt H. Waggoner, *Nathaniel Hawthorne.* "Pamphlets on American Writers." Minneapolis: University of Minnesota Press, 1962.

3. *The Scarlet Letter* has been called an allegory—a story in which the characters, objects, or places represent some abstract quality. (For example, a character may represent kindness or courage.) Identify representative characters, objects, and places and the qualities each represents. Do these representations remain constant throughout the novel, or do they change? Explain. *See also* Richard Chase, *The American Novel and Its Tradition.* Garden City, NY: Doubleday, 1957, and D.H. Lawrence, *Studies in Classic American Literature.* Garden City, NY: Doubleday, 1923.

4. Hester suffers as a consequence of breaking the adultery law. In what ways does she suffer? How does she compensate for the suffering that the community imposes on her? *See also* Edward Wagenknecht, "Characters in *The Scarlet Letter*," in Eileen Morey, ed., *Readings on The Scarlet Letter.* San Diego: Greenhaven Press, 1998.

5. In his meeting with Hester in the forest, Dimmesdale describes his life as "the torment of a seven years' cheat." What caused the torment for him? Why does he continue to live in secret as a "cheat"? *See also* Mark Van Doren, *Nathaniel Hawthorne.* New York: Viking, 1949, and Edward Wagenknecht, "Characters in *The Scarlet Letter*," In Eileen Morey, ed., *Readings on The Scarlet Letter.* San Diego: Greenhaven Press, 1998.

6. Dimmesdale says that Chillingworth's revenge is black. "He has violated, in cold blood, the sanctity of a human heart." What does Dimmesdale mean? What has Chillingworth done? Do you agree

that he committed a black, unpardonable sin? *See also* Hugo McPherson, *Hawthorne the Myth-Maker: A Study in Imagination.* Toronto: University of Toronto Press, 1969.

7. Many critics describe Pearl as a complex symbol; a few argue that she acts as a little girl would in her circumstances. Do you think she is a symbol, a little girl, or a combination of both? Cite examples to support your argument. *See also* Seymour L. Gross, ed., *A Scarlet Letter Handbook.* San Francisco: Wadsworth, 1960, and D.H. Lawrence, *Studies in Classic American Literature.* Garden City, NY: Doubleday, 1923.

8. Hawthorne explores the psychological effects of sin on the mind, heart, and spirit. By the end of the novel, what psychological effect has Hester and Dimmesdale's adultery had on Hester, Dimmesdale, Chillingworth, the wronged husband, and Pearl? *See also* John C. Gerber, ed., *Twentieth Century Interpretations of* The Scarlet Letter. Englewood Cliffs, NJ: Prentice-Hall, 1968, and Richard H. Millington, *Practicing Romance: Narrative Form and Cultural Engagements in Hawthorne's Fiction.* Princeton, NJ: Princeton University Press, 1992.

9. The forest, or wilderness as it is often called, plays an important part in *The Scarlet Letter.* Is it a symbol? Is it a special place? Does it have different meanings for different characters in the novel? Explain and cite examples. *See also* Terence Martin, *Nathaniel Hawthorne.* New York: Twayne, 1965, and Alison Easton, *The Making of the Hawthorne Subject.* Columbia: University of Missouri Press, 1996.

10. Religious beliefs are important in the Puritan community. What are the religious beliefs of the Puritans? How do Hester, Dimmesdale, and Chillingworth differ in their acceptance of these beliefs? *See also* Randall Stewart and Dorothy Bethurum, "History, Art, and Wisdom in *The Scarlet Letter*," in Clarice Swisher, ed., *Readings on Nathaniel Hawthorne.* San Diego: Greenhaven Press, 1996.

11. Hypocrisy is an important theme in *The Scarlet Letter.* Which major and minor characters are hypocrites, and which are not? Explain your decisions. *See also* Terence Martin, *Nathaniel Hawthorne.* New York: Twayne, 1965, and D.H. Lawrence, *Studies in Classic American Literature.* Garden City, NY: Doubleday, 1923.

12. Some critics argue that the three scaffold scenes serve as the structure on which the novel is built. Where do they occur in the story? What happens in each scene? Who is present? How do the scenes

mark changes in the development of Hester, Pearl, Dimmesdale, and Chillingworth? *See also* Terence Martin, *Nathaniel Hawthorne.* New York: Twayne, 1965, and John C. Gerber, *Twentieth Century Interpretations of* The Scarlet Letter. Englewood Cliffs, NJ: Prentice-Hall, 1968.

13. Hawthorne makes a distinction between Old England and New England. How does he characterize each? Which major character most closely identifies with the old world and which with the new? Why do you think Hester, Dimmesdale, and Chillingworth, all born in England, end their lives in New England, but Pearl, born in New England, moves permanently to Old England? *See also* Frederick Newberry, "Hawthorne Examines English Traditions," in Eileen Morcy, ed., *Readings on* The Scarlet Letter. San Diego: Greenhaven Press, 1998, and Michael Davitt Bell, "Old and New Worlds in *The Scarlet Letter,*" in *Readings on Nathaniel Hawthorne,* Clarice Swisher, ed., San Diego: Greenhaven Press, 1996.

14. Hawthorne uses colors, especially red and black in various shades and intensities, to convey meaning. Identify several excerpts using each color, and explain what the color contributes to the meaning of the passage. *See also* Richard Harter Fogle, *Hawthorne's Fiction: The Light and Dark.* Norman: University of Oklahoma Press, 1964.

# Appendix of Criticism

### *The Scarlet Letter*'s Grand Effects

The frivolous costume and brisk action of the story of fashionable life are easily depicted by the practised sketcher, but a work like *The Scarlet Letter* comes slowly upon the canvas, where passions are commingled and overlaid with the masterly elaboration with which the grandest effects are produced in pictorial composition and coloring. It is a distinction of such works that while they are acceptable to the many, they also surprise and delight the few who appreciate the nicest arrangement and the most high and careful finish. *The Scarlet Letter* will challenge consideration in the name of Art.

Rufus Wilmot Griswold, "The Writings of
Hawthorne," in *International Magazine,* 1851

## Hawthorne Compared with European Novelists

With all the care in point of style and authenticity which mark his lighter sketches, this genuine and unique romance may be considered as an artistic exposition of Puritanism as modified by New England colonial life. In truth to costume, local manners, and scenic features, *The Scarlet Letter* is as reliable as the best of [Sir Walter] Scott's novels; in the anatomy of human passion and consciousness it resembles the most effective of [Honoré de] Balzac's illustrations of Parisian or provincial life; while in developing bravely and justly the sentimental of the life it depicts, it is as true to humanity as [Charles] Dickens.

Henry Theodore Tuckerman, "The Prose Poet:
Nathaniel Hawthorne," in *Mental Portraits,*
G.P. Putnam's Sons, 1853

## Suspense Focused on Pictures of Human Nature

*The Scarlet Letter* is, on the English side of the water, perhaps the best known. It is so terrible in its pictures of diseased human nature as to produce most questionable delight. The reader's interest never flags for a moment. There is nothing of episode or digression. The author is always telling his one story with a concentration of energy which, as we can understand, must have made it impossible for him to deviate. The reader will certainly go on with it to the end very quickly, entranced, excited, shuddering, and at times almost wretched.

Anthony Trollope, "The Genius of Nathaniel
Hawthorne," in *North American Review* 129, 1879

## Too Much Symbolism

In *The Scarlet Letter* there is a great deal of symbolism; there is, I
think, too much. It is overdone at times, and becomes mechanical;
it ceases to be impressive, and grazes triviality. The idea of the
mystic *A* which the young minister finds imprinted upon his breast
and eating into his flesh, in sympathy with the embroidered badge
that Hester is condemned to wear, appears to me to be a case in
point. This suggestion should, I think, have been just made and
dropped; to insist upon it, and return to it, is to exaggerate the
weak side of the subject. Hawthorne returns to it constantly, plays
with it, and seems charmed by it; until at last the reader feels
tempted to declare that his employment of it is puerile.

Henry James, *Hawthorne,* from the
"English Men of Letters" series, 1880

## The Cultural History of Puritan America

*The Scarlet Letter* is about the cultural history of Puritan America, and the conflict between dominant and recessive qualities of
Puritanism more or less defined by 1649. . . . With his knowledge
of colonial American history, in conjunction with his considerable
knowledge of English history, Hawthorne again traces the growth
of the dominating forces of Puritanism: severity, rigidity, intoler-
ance, iconoclasm, militancy, and persecution. But he also explores
to a far greater extent than earlier the attractive but recessive
qualities of early Puritans that form a part of their English heritage: sympathy, charity, gaiety, communal celebration, respect
for tradition, and appreciation of art. These qualities—personi-
fied especially by Dimmesdale, Hester, and Pearl—are posed as alternatives to the dominant traits of the Puritan majority. . . .

The gentle side of Puritanism retreats as the militant side continually advances. Moreover, Hawthorne takes up in *The Scarlet
Letter* where he leaves off in "The Custom House," allying himself with an English ancestry whose aesthetic and spiritual traditions are pitted against those of his Puritan forebears, which
essentially survive among his contemporaries. While the dominant
values of the Puritans are not wholly those of nineteenth-century
Salemites, the recessive values in each century are nearly identical
as expressed through Hawthorne's self-projected narrator. The

majority parties of the seventeenth and nineteenth centuries are oppressive in their own ways, as they resist or fail to consider either the value of art or alternatives to the narrow Puritan tradition. The legacy of Puritan antipathy for artistic values survives in nineteenth-century descendants, even though religious zeal does not.

Frederick Newberry, *Hawthorne's Divided Loyalties: England and America in His Works,* Fairleigh Dickinson University Press, 1987

## *The Scarlet Letter* Is a Historical Novel

Hawthorne knew well the early history of New England and used it repeatedly as a source of literary material. His first American ancestor, William Hathorne, came over from England with John Winthrop in 1630, and later, as a magistrate of the Massachusetts Bay Colony, ordered the public whipping of a Quakeress. William's son, John, was a member of the Salem court that, in 1692, condemned to death those convicted of witchcraft. Hawthorne felt deeply his connection with these forebears. In the autobiographical essay "The Custom House," he spoke of himself as "their representative," and went on to say, "I hereby take shame upon myself for their sakes, and pray that any curse incurred by them . . . may be now and henceforth removed." Despite his disapproval of their bigotry and cruelty, he recognized the ancestral tie: "Strong traits of their nature," he said, "have intertwined themselves with mine." It might not be farfetched to think that the writing of *The Scarlet Letter* was, for Hawthorne, a kind of expiation of his ancestors' guilt. But whether this be true or not, few books have come so completely out of the inherited experience of the author.

*The Scarlet Letter* is, in a sense, a historical novel. The plot is the author's invention, and the four chief characters—Arthur Dimmesdale, Hester Prynne, Roger Chillingworth, Pearl—are fictitious persons. But the lesser characters—Governor Bellingham, the Reverend John Wilson, Mistress Hibbins, Master Brackett, the jailer—are historical figures prominent in the early annals of Boston. Details of setting and costume are faithfully rendered. The reader can assume that Mistress Hibbins' elaborate headdress, for example, is historically accurate; likewise, the market place, whose conspicuous features are the meeting house, the jail, and the scaffold; accurate, too, the ceremonies accompanying the Election Sermon, and the pervasive allusions to witchcraft; for Hawthorne was something of a research scholar in colonial New England history. Moreover, the plot itself, though invented, is based upon a historical form of punishment: Plymouth Colony, for example, passed a law in 1636 requiring that anyone guilty of adultery should "weare two Capitall letters viz. AD. cut out in cloth and sowed on theire upermost Garments on theire arme or backe; and if att any time they shalbee taken without the said letters whiles they are in the Gov'ment soe worn to bee forthwith taken and publickly whipt." Historians, in general, have made no objection to *The Scarlet Letter* as a picture of mid-seventeenth century Boston, except the qualification that the historical reality was probably somewhat less somber than Hawthorne's representation. If Hawthorne overemphasized the somberness, the reason is seen in the artistic fitness of such an emphasis in a "drama of guilt and sorrow": Hawthorne was a creative artist as well as a historian.

Randall Stewart and Dorothy Bethurum, *Classic American Fiction: Book Two,* Scott Foresman and Company, 1954

## The Characters Play Against a Fixed Puritan Background

*The Scarlet Letter* might have appeared without the character Mistress Hibbins and without, say, an account of Pearl's relations with the Puritan children. . . . Christian doctrine, the lore of witchcraft and black magic and alchemy, the nature and history of Puritan New England—these are given elements in *The Scarlet Letter;* they are not at issue. They form the substantial background, understood by both author and reader, against which to observe the characters as they confront the questions that are at issue—in this instance the breaking of moral and theological laws belonging to the background. This background serves for Hawthorne the same purpose the fixed social order of England, France, and Italy serves for [American novelist] Henry James. The initial sin of Hester Prynne and Arthur Dimmesdale precedes the opening of the first chapter and is not questioned by the characters or the author. Though Hester says that what they did had a consecration of its own, it is in her view a sin nevertheless and its consequences are inevitable. Similarly, in the final scaffold scene, the reader wanders out of the romance if he asks whether or not Dimmesdale has won salvation. His tentative answer to Hester's question whether they will meet in heaven is firmly within the context of seventeenth-century beliefs in Boston, not beliefs in the author's time or in a reader's time. The romance presents a psychological study, not a theological study, though the characters move within a pattern of fixed moral and theological beliefs. The integrity of the work requires this distinction.

Arlin Turner, *Nathaniel Hawthorne: A Biography*,
Oxford University Press, 1980

## The Puritan Past Suits a Psychological Romance

He wrote in a time that showed a strong interest in romantic histories, grand epics in which heroic explorers or military leaders moved through sublime scenes. And he, along with thousands of his countrymen, admired the historical romances of Sir Walter Scott and James Fenimore Cooper. He was well aware of the shallow characterization in these works, but he resolved to use the conventional forms as a way of writing a new kind of fiction. Most of the popular writers of romance had been content to treat characters as stereotypes: the dashing, warm-hearted hero who was sympathetic to nature and who obeyed natural laws was pitted against a heartless, intellectual villain who defended the letter of the law. In this scheme the complexity of human character was usually suggested, not within one person, but by contrasts between other groups of simple types, such as the two heroines: the fair lady, whose moderate feelings pointed the way to true values; and the dark lady, who was either too intellectual or too passionate to be a fit mate for the hero. Hawthorne accepted such conventions and transformed them. He called his fiction psychological romance, and he declared that he would "burrow into the depths of our common nature." He used the historical romance and its conventions to achieve a deeper psychological intensity than any of his predecessors had accomplished. And, of course, in turning to the past, he turned to the Puritan past.

There are several reasons why this choice was remarkably appropriate. Hawthorne, like his ancestors, was preoccupied with the moral life, with questions of responsibility and motivation, and with the moral and psychological effects of sin or misfortune. He once spoke apologetically of his "inveterate habit of allegory." In writing about the Puritans he was able to bring his readers into a world of people who considered their own lives allegorical. Hawthorne believed that the romance, unlike the novel, did not have to restrict itself to the probable; so long as the romance was true to what he called the truth of the human heart, it had every right to mingle the marvelous and the real. Romances, he said, ought to be written and read by moonlight or by the dim light of the coal fire, in an atmosphere that brings the reader into "a neutral territory, somewhere between the real world and fairyland, where the actual and imaginary may meet and each imbue itself with the nature of the other." . . . When Hawthorne chose to write about seventeenth-century Boston, whose people really believed in devils and witches and in a jealous God who intervened in their daily affairs, he chose a community that recognized no clear line between the real world and what we might call fairyland; he chose a community in which it was especially difficult to distinguish between the actual and the imaginary.

David Levin, *The American Novel: From James Fenimore Cooper to William Faulkner,* edited by Wallace Stegner, Basic Books, 1965

## The Novel's Characters Balance Opposing Forces

In a literature branded by the mark of the misogynist, . . . Hester Prynne is the first authentic American heroine. And if Hawthorne was constrained by inheritance and temperament to respect "the whole dismal severity of the Puritanic code of law," his own deepest sympathies were still extended (as in the similar cases of his two great contemporaries [Melville and Whitman] to the wild votaries of joy. It is just this balance of opposing forces in the novelist's characters—and in his own heart—which makes *The Scarlet Letter* so impressive today. Yes, that; and the brooding note of pity with which Hawthorne viewed those heroic women who were sacrificed, whether by sacred edict or social convenience, on the altar of masculine institutions.

Maxwell Geismar, from the 1955 Afterword to *The Scarlet Letter,* Washington Square Press, 1972

## The Shifting Voice of the Narrator

The narrator's voice is an additional complicating factor in this drama of character, place, and event, and one means of introducing moral analysis into the novel without giving that voice complete authority. The narrator is not identical to the Surveyor/authorial persona in "The Custom-House," let alone to Hawthorne himself. His function is neither simply that of expositor and stage manager, nor that of didacticism's judge and moral spokesman. He is one of the many strands of the novel, out of which is spun a web of confrontations, questions, and doubts. His descriptions always tend to slide into multiple interpretation. Neither does the narrator present himself as the foreknowing oracle of truth, fully in control of his tale. Instead of a story recalled, there is often a sense of unanticipated events jolting him into immediate reaction. Doubt is created in a rush of proffered alternatives (for instance, Hester's motives for staying), with proliferating conditionals (such as "it might be," "it is probable," "Hester saw or seemed to see," "she felt or fancied"). These clamor impossibly for resolution—impossibly, because of the difficulty of ever knowing any character fully, let alone settling the clash of competing needs and desires.

The narrator, as a liberal democrat trying to transform what he regards as an unsavory seventeenth-century tale of immorality and tyranny into something his nineteenth-century audience can accept without disturbing too much its present notions of gender relations, does not keep a constant position throughout. Challenged by the story, he struggles with his own nineteenth-century social indoctrination. A gap gradually widens between the narrative voice and other possible responses to events, as the tale pushes against the restraining narrative framework and the reader is forced to see the deficiencies of the narrator's responses and the narrator's own failure to see these inadequacies. . . .

What is disturbing is not his actual inconclusiveness (which is surely understandable) but his continuing desire for neat answers, particularly when this is sought with a sentimental inflection uncharacteristic of the rest of the novel (as in his speculation that, in the afterlife, Dimmesdale and Chillingworth may find their antipathy "transmuted into golden love"). The handling of narrative focalization also ensures that the reader's perspective is in a marked state of constant change and confusion, so that the reader not only experiences the many contradictory viewpoints but also is made aware that the narrator at times obscures our view of a character in the interests of making his own point, or more simply seems not to have the imaginative power to envisage his protagonists' thoughts. There is a conscious deliberation about the way the center of consciousness is moved from character to character, sometimes so that the reader is simultaneously within and outside a character—for example, Dimmesdale on the midnight scaffold, or Hester looking toward her future at the beginning of chapter 5. One device in particular keeps readers on their toes. Occasionally a view of events is presented without introduction so that it appears to be that of the narrator, only to be then followed by a phrase revealing it to be instead one of the characters' possibly idiosyncratic ideas. Tempted by the momentary ambiguity of omniscient narration, the reader then learns that what seemed objectively true or at least validated by the narrator is something only subjectively believed. Indeed, at times it never becomes clear whose thoughts we have been given. Examples of this temporary syntactical ambiguity can be found first in the opening description of Pearl, where two sentences apparently stating the incontrovertible fact of Hester's guilt are followed by, "Yet these thoughts affected Hester Prynne"; and second in the motives given for Dimmesdale's vigil on the scaffold, where it is not clear until the beginning of the subsequent paragraph that the vivid portrait of his sin is a record of Dimmesdale's thoughts rather than the apparently more authoritative narrator's: "And thus . . . Mr. Dimmesdale was overcome with a great horror of mind.". . . .

This device is important because it results in a constant tension between sharing sympathetically and directly with a character or the narrator, and being aware of the limits of such subjective vision and claims. A precarious sense of events is pieced together out of this range of experience, thought, and commentary. Such an unstable narrative mode suggests the attempt both to "sympathize" in a *Mosses* sense and a desire to step back from this to seek a wider pattern of meaning.

Allison Easton, *The Making of the Hawthorne Subject,* University Missouri Press, 1966

## The Frame and Balanced Structure of *The Scarlet Letter*

The structural plan of *The Scarlet Letter* is one of its most beautiful and artistic qualities. . . . The introduction and the conclusion constitute a kind of frame around the story of Hester Prynne. It is true that this frame is not built in quite the same way as many of Hawthorne's frames are, and that it is not perfectly balanced. But its two sections are as much separated from the main story as they are related to it; and I think we may treat them either as a structural part of the story or as a frame. For the sake of simplifying the analysis of the novel's structure, I have chosen to think of "The Custom House" and "Conclusion" as a frame, apart from the story itself.

When we make this separation, the pattern of the story becomes clear and beautiful. It is built around the scaffold. At the beginning, in the middle, and at the end of the story the scaffold is the dominating point. Just as it literally rises above the market-place, so does it structurally rise out of the novel's plan and attribute pattern to it. In chapter two, after the very short first chapter, Hester is taken up on the scaffold. In chapter twelve, the middle chapter (when we omit the concluding chapter), Dimmesdale mounts the scaffold. In chapter twenty-three, the last (omitting the conclusion), Dimmesdale takes Hester and Pearl up there with him. These three incidents are, in every sense, the high points of the novel. The middle chapter, number twelve, tends to divide the story into two parts (or three parts, counting this middle chapter). This division is logical when we realize that up to chapter twelve neither the reader nor Chillingworth is certain that Dimmesdale is the father of little Pearl; after chapter twelve, there can be no doubt.

There is more to the pattern than this two-fold division. The scaffold, in Boston, stands in the market-place. The setting of the first three and the last three chapters is the market-place. In the first three chapters, Hester's ignominy is established. The last three chapters build up to and include Dimmesdale's victory over Chillingworth. Thus these two groups of chapters are set-off from the remainder of the story by locale as well as by function. The chapters between the first three and the middle one fall nicely into two groups of five and three chapters each. The group of five—chapters four through eight—deal chiefly with Pearl and Hester and describe Hester's struggles in the community. The group of three—chapters nine, ten, and eleven—deal with Chillingworth and Dimmesdale and show Chillingworth gaining the minister's confidence and digging out his secret. There are also eight chapters between chapter twelve and the last three, and they, too, fall into two groups of three and five chapters each. The group of three—chapters thirteen, fourteen, and fifteen—deal with Hester and Pearl again and indicate Hester's improved condition both in the community and within herself. The group of five—chapters sixteen through twenty—show the partial reunion of Hester and Dimmesdale and their growing resistance to Chillingworth's power.

From Leland Schubert, *Hawthorne the Artist: Fine-Art Devices in Fiction,* Chapel Hill, 1944.

## Dramatic Irony Heightens the Novel's Intensity

The intensity of *The Scarlet Letter* comes in part from a sustained and rigorous dramatic irony, or irony of situation. This irony arises naturally from the theme of "secret sin," or concealment. "Show freely of your worst," says Hawthorne; the action of *The Scarlet Letter* arises from the failure of Dimmesdale and Chillingworth to do so. The minister hides his sin, and Chillingworth hides his identity. This concealment affords a constant drama. There is the irony of Chapter III, "The Recognition," in which Chillingworth's ignorance is suddenly and blindingly reversed. Separated from his wife by many vicissitudes, he comes upon her as she is dramatically exposed to public infamy. From his instantaneous decision, symbolized by the lifting of his finger to his lips to hide his tie to her, he precipitates the further irony of his sustained hypocrisy.

In the same chapter Hester is confronted with her fellow-adulterer, who is publicly called upon to persuade her as her spiritual guide to reveal his identity. Under the circumstances the situation is highly charged, and his words have a double meaning—one to the onlookers, another far different to Hester and the speaker himself. "'If thou feelest it to be for thy soul's peace, and that thy earthly punishment will therefore be made more effectual to salvation, I charge thee to speak out the name of thy fellow-sinner and fellow-sufferer!'"

From this scene onward Chillingworth, by living a lie, arouses a constant irony, which is also an ambiguity. With a slight shift in emphasis all his actions can be given a very different interpretation. Seen purely from without, it would be possible to regard him as completely blameless. Hester expresses this ambiguity in Chapter IV, after he has ministered to her sick baby, the product of her faithlessness, with tenderness and skill. "'Thy acts are like mercy,'" said Hester, bewildered and appalled. "'But thy words interpret thee as a terror!'" Masquerading as a physician, he becomes to Dimmesdale a kind of attendant fiend, racking the minister's soul with constant anguish. Yet outwardly he has done him nothing but good. "'What evil have I done the man?' asked Roger Chillingworth again. 'I tell thee, Hester Prynne, the richest fee that ever physician earned from monarch could not have bought such care as I have wasted on this miserable priest!'" Even when he closes the way to escape by proposing to take passage on the same ship with the fleeing lovers, it is possible to consider the action merely friendly. His endeavor at the end to hold Dimmesdale back from the saving scaffold is from one point of view reasonable and friendlike, although he is a devil struggling to snatch back an escaping soul. "'All shall be well! Do not blacken your fame, and perish in dishonor! I can yet save you! Would you bring infamy on your sacred profession?'" Only when Dimmesdale has successfully resisted does Chillingworth openly reveal his purposes. With the physician the culminating irony is that in seeking to damn Dimmesdale he has himself fallen into damnation. As he says in a moment of terrible self-knowledge, "'A mortal man, with once a human heart, has become a fiend for his especial torment!'" The effect is of an Aristotelian reversal, where a conscious and deep-laid purpose brings about totally unforeseen and opposite results. Chillingworth's relations with Dimmesdale have the persistent fascination of an almost absolute knowledge and power working their will with a helpless victim, a fascination which is heightened by the minister's awareness of an evil close beside him which he cannot place. "All this was accomplished with a subtlety so perfect that the minister, though he had constantly a dim perception of some evil influence watching over him, could never gain a knowledge of its actual nature." It is a classic situation wrought out to its fullest potentialities, in which the reader cannot help sharing the perverse pleasure of the villain.

From the victim's point of view the irony is still deeper, perhaps because we can participate still more fully in his response to it. Dimmesdale, a "remorseful hypocrite," is forced to live a perpetual lie in public. His own considerable talents for self-torture are supplemented by the situation as well as by the devoted efforts of Chillingworth. His knowledge is an agony. His conviction of sin is in exact relationship to the reverence in which his parishioners hold him. He grows pale and meager—it is the asceticism of a saint on earth; his effectiveness as a minister grows with his despair; he confesses the truth in his sermons, but transforms it "into the veriest falsehood" by the generality of his avowal and merely increases the adoration of his flock; every effort deepens his plight, since he will not—until the end—make the effort of complete self-revelation. His great election-day sermon prevails through anguish of heart; to his listeners divinely inspired, its power comes from its undertone of suffering, "the complaint of a human heart, sorrow-laden, perchance guilty, telling its secret, whether of guilt or sorrow, to the great heart of mankind. . . ." While Chillingworth at last reveals himself fully, Dimmesdale's secret is too great to be wholly laid bare. His utmost efforts are still partially misunderstood, and "highly respectable witnesses" interpret his death as a culminating act of holiness and humility.

Richard Harter Fogle, *Hawthornes Fiction: The Light and Dark,* University of Oklahoma Press, 1964

## *The Scarlet Letter* Is a Tragedy

In nothing that Hawthorne wrote are the tragic possibilities of the theme more richly and intensely realized than in "The Scarlet Letter." What makes the outcome of its events so pitiful and terrible is not simply that a great sin has had its retribution, but that the harmony of several related lives has been fatally jangled, that they have all been set at odds with the general purposes of the life about them, that all the fair potentialities of personal development have miscarried grievously and come to nothing. When we first hear of the embroidered letter shining on Hester Prynne's bosom, as she stands at the prison door with her child in her arms, it is to be told that the letter "had the effect of a spell, taking her out of the ordinary relations with humanity, and enclosing her in a sphere by herself." It is not for the intrinsic flagrance of the sin she has committed, but for the waywardness and irregularity of all wrongdoing, that she is punished; and the penalty is made to suit the offense, since Hester Prynne can never regain her innocent and normal status among men. In expiation of what she has done, she may adopt the rôle of a sister of charity, and thus come to have a certain part to perform in the world: "in all her intercourse with society, however, there was nothing that made her feel as if she belonged to it. Every gesture, every word, and even the silence of those with whom she came in contact, implied, and often expressed, that she was banished, and as much alone as if she inhabited another sphere, or communicated with the common nature by other organs and senses than the rest of human kind." In consequence of this alienation, the luxuriance and warmth of her personality undergo a kind of blight, and become austerity, coldness, and a rigid strength. Passion and feeling give way, in the movement of her life, to thought; and her thinking itself becomes bolder and more speculative, expressive not so much of her whole being as of a specialized and "unwomanly" function. At length she loses her clear sense of human realities—loses it so far as to suppose that she and Dimmesdale can achieve happiness by mere escape from the dangers and difficulties that beset them separately. No wonder Roger Chillingworth, in their interview on the edge of the forest, is moved to cry out, "Woman, I could wellnigh pity thee! . . . Thou hadst great elements. Peradventure, hadst thou met earlier with a better love than mine, this evil had not been. *I pity thee, for the good that has been wasted in thy nature!*"

Frustration like that which falls to the lot of Hester Prynne is the punishment of the man who has shared her guilt; and Dimmesdale is made to suffer even more atrociously than she because he has deepened his original wrongdoing by the secrecy with which he has invested it. This cuts him off still more effectually from the redemptive force of normal human relations. "There was an air about this young minister," we are told when he first appears, "as of a being who felt himself quite astray and at a loss in the pathway of human existence, and could only be at ease in some seclusion of his own." His noblest faculties and highest purposes seem engaged in the concealment of what he has done; the reverence in which he is held by his parishioners, and the pure spiritual influence he exercises upon them, are specious voices pleading against confession. But in all this there is too large an element of the unpardonable sin, too abject a surrender to spiritual pride; and the minister gradually discovers how deadly is its effect upon his moral world.

It is the unspeakable misery of a life so false as his, that it steals the pith and substance out of whatever realities there are around us, and which were meant by Heaven to be the spirit's joy and nutriment. To the untrue man, the whole universe is false,—it is impalpable,—it shrinks to nothing within his grasp.

In such a world, the fruits of personal character cannot ripen; and Dimmesdale's nature, like Hester's, is finally perverted and vitiated by the central falsity of his life. His refined spirituality becomes the instrument for a diseased self-persecution; his spiritual insight turns into a loathsome apprehension of the evil in other men's breasts. As he returns through the town after his interview with Hester in the forest, Dimmesdale is tempted at every step to perpetrate some monstrous impropriety of speech or act—the symbol of a moral sense gone hopelessly awry. Of this disastrous process there can be but one fit culmination, and that is reached and realized by the minister's public self-exposure and death. His own breast has been seared by the scarlet letter!

Neither Hester Prynne nor Dimmesdale, however, is represented as the greatest sinner of the drama, and their punishments are less terrible than that of the third chief personage. The pride of the detached intellect is Roger Chillingworth's error, and it is this, not the wayward passion of the other two, that lies at the very root of the whole tragedy.

Newton Arvin, *Hawthorne,* Russell & Russell, 1961

## Hawthorne's Use of Color and Light Images

In the three short paragraphs that make up his opening chapter Hawthorne introduces the three chief symbols that will serve to give structure to the story on the thematic level, hints at the fourth, and starts two of the chief lines of imagery. The opening sentence suggests the darkness ("sad-colored," "gray"), the rigidity ("oak," "iron"), and the aspiration ("steeple-crowned") of the people "amongst whom religion and law were almost identical." Later sentences add "weatherstains," "a yet darker aspect," and "gloomy" to the suggestions already begun through color imagery. The closing words of the chapter make the metaphorical use of color explicit: Hawthorne hopes that a wild rose beside the prison door may serve "to symbolize some sweet moral blossom, that may be found along the track, or relieve the darkening close of a tale of human frailty and sorrow.". . .

The extremes of Mr. Wilson's "light" and Chillingworth's "blackness" meet not only in the gray of Hester's dress and the Puritan hats, and in the indeterminate drabness of the Puritan clothing, but also in the ambiguous suggestions of red. Images of color, and of light and shade, are more numerous than any other images in the novel. Readers have always been aware that Hawthorne has used these images "artistically," and sometimes that he has used them "expressively"; yet precisely what they express and how they express it have never, even in the extended treatments of the subject, been adequately analyzed. Some of them Hawthorne makes explicitly symbolic, others seem obscurely to be so, while still others resist every effort at translation into abstract terms. . . . I think it will prove useful as a preliminary to later analysis to distinguish among three ways in which images of color and light and shade appear in the novel.

There is, first, the pure sensory image used literally [with exact meaning, factual], not figuratively [based on figures of speech, metaphorical], though the literalness of its use will not destroy whatever intrinsic symbolic value it may have. Second, there is the color or shade of light or darkness that must be taken literally but that also has explicit symbolic value. Finally, there is the image that has only, or chiefly, symbolic value, so that it cannot be taken literally.

Wyatt Howe Waggoner, Hawthorne: A Critical Study, Harvard University Press, 1955

## Love and Hate Equally Affect Unaware Characters

The last developments of plot in *The Scarlet Letter* approach the "mythic level" which redemption-minded critics love to discover, but the myth is wholly secular and worldly. Pearl, who has hitherto been a "messenger of anguish" to her mother, is emotionally transformed as she kisses Dimmesdale on the scaffold. "A spell was broken. The great scene of grief, in which the wild infant bore a part, had developed all her sympathies; and as her tears fell upon her father's cheek, they were the pledge that she would grow up amid human joy and sorrow, nor for ever do battle with the world, but be a woman in it." Thanks to Chillingworth's bequest—for Chillingworth, too, finds that a spell is broken when Dimmesdale confesses, and he is capable of at least one generous act before he dies—Pearl is made "the richest heiress of her day, in the New World." At last report she has become the wife of a European nobleman and is living very happily across the sea. This grandiose and perhaps slightly whimsical epilogue has one undeniable effect on the reader: it takes him as far as possible from the scene and spirit of Dimmesdale's farewell. Pearl's immense wealth, her noble title, her lavish and impractical gifts to Hester, and of course her successful escape from Boston all serve to disparage the Puritan sense of reality. From this distance we look back to Dimmesdale's egocentric confession, not as a moral example which Hawthorne would like us to follow, but as the last link in a chain of compulsion that has now been relaxed.

To counterbalance this impression we have the case of Hester, for whom the drama on the scaffold can never be completely over. After raising Pearl in a more generous atmosphere she voluntarily returns to Boston to resume, or rather to begin, her state of penitence. We must note, however, that this penitence seems to be devoid of theological content; Hester has returned because Boston and the scarlet letter offer her "a more real life" than she could find elsewhere, even with Pearl. This simply confirms Hawthorne's emphasis on the irrevocability of guilty acts. And though Hester is now selfless and humble, it is not because she believes in Christian submissiveness but because all passion has been spent. To the women who seek her help "in the continually recurring trials of wounded, wasted, wronged, misplaced, or erring and sinful passion," Hester does not disguise her conviction that women are pathetically misunderstood in her society. She assures her wretched friends that at some later period "a new truth would be revealed, in order to establish the whole relation between man and woman on a surer ground of mutual happiness." Hawthorne may or may not believe the prediction, but it has a retrospective importance in *The Scarlet Letter*. Hawthorne's characters originally acted in ignorance of passion's strength and persistence, and so they became its slaves.

"It is a curious subject of observation and inquiry," says Hawthorne at the end, "whether hatred and love be not the same thing at bottom. Each, in its utmost development, supposes a high degree of intimacy and heart-knowledge; each renders one individual dependent for the food of his affections and spiritual life upon another; each leaves the passionate lover, or the no less passionate hater, forlorn and desolate by the withdrawal of his object." These penetrating words remind us that the tragedy of *The Scarlet Letter* has chiefly sprung, not from Puritan society's imposition of false social ideals on the three main characters, but from their own inner world of frustrated desires. Hester, Dimmesdale, and Chillingworth have been ruled by feelings only half perceived, much less understood and regulated by consciousness; and these feelings, as Hawthorne's bold equation of love and hatred implies, successfully resist translation into terms of good and evil. Hawthorne does not leave us simply with the Sunday-school lesson that we should "be true," but with a tale of passion through which we glimpse the ruined wall—the terrible certainty that, as Freud put it, the ego is not master in its own house. It is this intuition that enables Hawthorne to reach a tragic vision worthy of the name: to see to the bottom of his created characters, to understand the inner necessity of everything they do, and thus to pity and forgive them in the very act of laying bare their weaknesses.

John C. Gerber, Twentieth Century Interpetations<br>of the Scarlet Letter, Prentice-Hall, 1968

## Hawthorne's Handling of the Harmful Effects of Patriarchal Culture

That Pearl never speaks at the end of this romance implies, first, how strongly Hawthorne believed that the truths she had to tell had not yet been heard in America, that patriarchy and patriarchal language still controlled and limited the minds of his audience. It also suggests how constrained he felt by those same cultural limitations and by the implications of his own "authority." We must remember that, from the beginning, Hawthorne identified not with Pearl but with Hester, that is, with Hester's otherness, with her victimization and her flawed psychology. Like Hester in the forest scene, he had also chosen to authorize others' speech and actions, and like Hester at the end, he must admit to living a "real life" in New England, where the truthful language of a Pearl was still "unknown," still a hopeful fiction. Finally, there is a strong sense at the end of this book that if, like Hester, he can do no positive good in bringing about change, at least he will do no more harm. He will not project his authority into the future by putting words into Pearl's mouth. He will only counsel Americans as best he might—and by personal example—about the harmful effects of patriarchal culture on individual minds and on language.

Cynthia S. Jordan, "Inhabiting the Second Story: Hawthorne's Houses," in *Second Stories: The Politics of Language, Form, and Gender in Early American Fictions,* University of North Carolina Press, 1989

## The Power of Shame

Hawthorne sets his scene to maximize the agony of shaming. Displayed on a scaffold in broad daylight, Hester stands before public gaze for hours wearing the badge of shame, holding her sin-born child, and then is subjected to public inquisition into most intimate matters. The Puritan custom of public exposure of sexual sinners allows Hawthorne to introduce Hester with shame rather than guilt or penitence, a strategy that aligns our sympathy with her and against the Puritans. Shame, more primitive than guilt, and less a product of society and the superego, is more readily mobilized for empathic purposes. Says the narrator, "There can be no outrage, methinks, against our common nature . . . no outrage more flagrant than to forbid the culprit to hide his face for shame; as it was the essence of this punishment to do." Hester cannot hide her face from the stares of the hostile crowd; rather, from among these stares she identifies the coldest, most unloving of them all—that of her husband.

On this same scaffold Dimmesdale, privileged to enjoy subtler sublimations of his sexuality than is Hester, both dreads and de-

sires to expose his own offenses. For him, too, the merciless prob-
ing of a single totally interested but coldhearted observer is more
agonizing than the gaze of impersonal multitudes. Having lived
under the same roof with Chillingworth, having been watched
covertly (behind his back, as it were), so intently as to have become the principal object of the physician's highly sexualized
scrutiny, and having himself come to practice self-flagellation as
penance, Dimmesdale has more than mere adultery to expiate. By
the conclusion of the novel he has far surpassed that first and
simpler sin which earlier he had duplicitously exhorted Hester
to reveal "if it be for [her] soul's good." Now a master of transformations, he attempts ambiguous self-exposure in the subtext
or scarcely audible undertone of his final public address, the Election Sermon. Because this submerged meaning is audible only to
Hester, who knows it already, he restates his insufficiently publi-
cized message more openly by exposing his bare bosom, which
again can be read only by those who already understand. He
makes his final and also misinterpreted statement by embracing
Pearl only moments before death enables him to hide his face for-
ever. One motive for all this dubious public exposure is to escape
the torturing scrutiny of Chillingworth. Paradoxically, even ambiguous or duplicitous publication of shame distributes it and
helps dilute its corrosive sting.

Gloria Erlich, *Family Themes in Hawthorne's Fiction: The
Teenacious Web,* Rutgers University Press, 1984

# Chronology

**1621**
William Bradford is chosen as governor of Plymouth Plantation.

**1630**
John Winthrop's group of Puritans establishes Massachusetts Bay Colony; William Hathorne comes to Salem, Massachusetts.

**1637**
Anne Hutchinson is tried over her repudiation of the role of the Puritan minister.

**1692**
Nineteen residents of Salem, Massachusetts, are executed for witchcraft; Puritan judge John Hathorne presides at trials.

**1801**
Hawthorne's parents, Nathaniel Hawthorne and Elizabeth Manning, marry on August 2.

**1802**
Hawthorne's sister Elizabeth is born.

**1804**
Nathaniel Hawthorne is born on July 4.

**1808**
Captain Nathaniel Hathorne dies, and Hawthorne's sister Maria Louisa is born; James Madison is elected president.

**1816**
James Monroe is elected president; the Hawthornes move to Maine.

**1818**
Hawthorne is brought back to Salem to prepare for college.

**1821**
Hawthorne enters Bowdoin College.

**1825**
Hawthorne graduates from Bowdoin College.

**1828**
Hawthorne publishes *Fanshawe*.

**1830**
Hawthorne publishes first tales anonymously in *Salem Gazette* and in the *Token,* an annual Boston publication.

**1831–1837**
Hawthorne publishes twenty-two tales in the *Token*.

## 1835
Hawthorne publishes eight tales in the *New England Magazine*.

## 1836
Martin Van Buren is elected president; Hawthorne edits the *American Magazine of Useful and Entertaining Knowledge*.

## 1837
Hawthorne publishes *Twice-Told Tales*.

## 1838
Hawthorne becomes engaged to Sophia Peabody.

## 1839–1840
Hawthorne works at Boston Custom House.

## 1841
Overland migration to California starts; Hawthorne publishes *Grandfather's Chair;* Hawthorne joins Brook Farm Community; President William Harrison dies and is succeeded by John Tyler.

## 1842
Hawthorne marries Sophia Peabody in Boston, and the newlyweds move to Old Manse; Hawthorne publishes enlarged edition of *Twice-Told Tales*.

## 1844
First message is sent by Samuel Morse's telegraph; Edgar Allan Poe publishes "The Raven;" Hawthorne's daughter Una is born.

## 1845
Texas is annexed by United States; the Hawthornes move to Salem; Henry David Thoreau moves to Walden Pond.

## 1846
Hawthorne's son Julian is born; Hawthorne publishes *Mosses from an Old Manse;* Hawthorne begins work at the Salem Custom House.

## 1849
Hawthorne loses job at Salem Custom House; Hawthorne's mother Elizabeth dies.

## 1850
Hawthorne publishes *The Scarlet Letter* and moves his family to Lenox, Massachusetts.

## 1851
Hawthorne's daughter Rose is born; Hawthorne publishes *The House of the Seven Gables* and the third edition of *Twice-Told Tales;* the Hawthornes leave Lenox; Herman Melville publishes *Moby Dick*.

## 1852
Hawthorne publishes *Blithedale Romance* and *A Wonder Book for Girls and Boys;* Hawthorne's friend Franklin Pierce is elected president; the Hawthornes move to Wayside in Concord, Massachusetts.

## 1853
Hawthorne's sister Maria Louisa is killed in a boat accident; Hawthorne publishes *Tanglewood Tales;* President Pierce appoints Hawthorne to post of consul at Liverpool, England.

## 1857
Hawthorne resigns Liverpool consulship.

## 1857–1859
The Hawthornes live in Italy.

## 1859
Hawthorne returns to England and finishes *The Marble Faun.*

## 1860
Hawthorne publishes *The Marble Faun;* the Hawthornes return to America.

## 1863
Hawthorne publishes *Our Old Home.*

## 1864
Hawthorne dies at Plymouth, New Hampshire, and is buried at Concord, Massachusetts.

# Works Consulted

## Major Editions of *The Scarlet Letter*

*Classic American Fiction: Edgar Allan Poe, Nathaniel Hawthorne, Herman Melville, Henry James.* Eds. Randall Stewart and Dorothy Bethurum. Chicago: Scott, Foresman, 1954.

Nathaniel Hawthorne, *The Scarlet Letter: A Romance.* Intro. by Nina Boym. Notes by Thomas E. Connolly. New York: Penguin, 1962.

———, *The Scarlet Letter.* New York: Avenel Books, 1985.

———, *The Scarlet Letter.* Intro. and Notes by Brian Harding. New York: Oxford University Press, 1990.

———, *The Scarlet Letter.* New York: Washington Square Press, 1994.

———, *The Scarlet Letter.* New York: Barnes and Noble, 1998.

## Also by Nathaniel Hawthorne

Newton Arvin, ed., *The Heart of Hawthorne's Journals.* Boston: Houghton Mifflin, 1929. Selected entries from Hawthorne's journals from 1835 to 1862, divided into two- to five-year time units, each with a brief introduction by Arvin.

Malcolm Cowley, ed., *The Portable Hawthorne.* New York: Viking, 1948. Contains *The Scarlet Letter* and excerpts from *American Notebooks, English Notebooks,* and Hawthorne's letters, plus an introduction by Malcolm Cowley.

Nathaniel Hawthorne, *The American Notebooks.* Ed. Randall Stewart. New Haven, CT: Yale University Press, 1932.

Nathaniel Hawthorne, *The Blithedale Romance.* Intro. by Arlin Turner. New York: W.W. Norton, 1958.

Nathaniel Hawthorne, *The House of the Seven Gables.* Intro. by Van Wyck Brooks. New York: The Heritage Press, 1935.

Nathaniel Hawthorne, *The Marble Faun: or, The Romance of Monte Beni.* Columbus: Ohio State University Press, 1968.

Nathaniel Hawthorne, *Mosses from an Old Manse.* Boston: Houghton Mifflin, 1882.

Nathaniel Hawthorne, *Twice Told Tales.* Intro. by Roy Harvey Pearce. New York: Dutton Everyman's Library, 1967.

## Biographical Information

Newton Arvin, *Hawthorne*. New York: Russell & Russell, 1961. A personal narrative beginning with Hawthorne's college days and concluding with his funeral. Arvin's text is generously supplemented with excerpts from Hawthorne's letters and journals.

Gloria C. Erlich, *Family Themes and Hawthorne's Fiction: The Tenacious Web*. New Brunswick, NJ: Rutgers University Press, 1984. Focuses on early family relationships and other experiences that serve as psychological and experiential background for the themes, plots, and characters that recur in Hawthorne's works.

Randall Stewart, *Nathaniel Hawthorne: A Biography*. New Haven, CT: Yale University Press, 1948. A thorough biography beginning with Hawthorne's ancestors and ending with an account of his family and the publication of his collected works after his death. Almost no commentary on Hawthorne's works.

Arlin Turner, *Nathaniel Hawthorne: A Biography*. New York: Oxford University Press, 1980. A detailed account of Hawthorne's life from his birth to his death. Turner devotes whole chapters to major works and the circumstances of their writing.

## Literary Criticism

Sculley Bradley, Richmond Croom Beatty, and E. Hudson Long, *The American Tradition in Literature*, 3rd ed., vol. 1. New York: W.W. Norton, 1967. An anthology of works from American literature from colonial times through the Romantic period. The editors provide critical introductions to the literary works as well as biographical information about the authors.

Richard Chase, *The American Novel and Its Tradition*. Garden City, NY: Doubleday, 1957. The chapter on *The Scarlet Letter* reviews the critical approaches—allegory, history, myth—taken by other critics and presents arguments for and against them.

Alison Easton, *The Making of the Hawthorne Subject*. Columbia: University of Missouri Press, 1996. In showing that Hawthorne's work evolved in a gradual, developmental manner, the author devotes chapters on each stage, an especially thorough one on *The Scarlet Letter*.

Norman Foerster, ed., *American Prose and Poetry*, 3rd ed. Boston: Houghton Mifflin, 1947. An anthology of American literature. Editor includes background information on each period in American literature and a critical introduction to each author represented in the anthology.

Richard Harter Fogle, *Hawthorne's Fiction: The Light and the Dark*. Norman: University of Oklahoma Press, 1964. The chapter on *The Scarlet Letter* analyzes the images of light and dark and relates them to the themes.

John C. Gerber, ed., *Twentieth Century Interpretations of The Scarlet Letter: A Collection of Critical Essays*. Englewood Cliffs, NJ: Prentice-Hall, 1968. Critical essays organized into four categories—background, form, techniques, and interpretations.

Seymour L. Gross, ed., *A Scarlet Letter Handbook*. San Francisco: Wadsworth, 1960. Critical essays organized into four categories—theme, characters, symbolism, and structure. Also contains a summary of Hawthorne's writing before *The Scarlet Letter.*

D.H. Lawrence, *Studies in Classic American Literature*. Garden City, NY: Doubleday, 1923. A good source for questions about *The Scarlet Letter* as allegory and myth.

Terence Martin, *Nathaniel Hawthorne*. New York: Twayne, 1965. Contains a short biography of Hawthorne and analysis of the scaffold scenes and Hawthorne's ambiguity.

Hugo McPherson, *Hawthorne the Myth-Maker: A Study in Imagination*. Toronto: University of Toronto Press, 1969. The chapter on *The Scarlet Letter* discusses the Puritan Community, Chillingworth, and Hester as forces operating in the novel.

Richard H. Millington, *Practicing Romance: Narrative Form and Cultural Engagements in Hawthorne's Fiction*. Princeton, NJ: Princeton University Press, 1992. Discusses the theme of sin and guilt and Hester's efforts at coping.

Eileen Morey, ed., *Readings on* The Scarlet Letter. San Diego: Greenhaven Press, 1998. A short biography of Hawthorne and excerpts from major critics organized into chapters on structure and style, characters, and major themes.

Alfred S. Reid, *The Yellow Ruff &* The Scarlet Letter: *A Source of Hawthorne's Novel*. Gainsville: University of Florida Press, 1955. Traces elements in the plot, characters, setting, style, and conclusion to the murder of Sir Thomas Overbury in the Tower of London in 1613.

Clarice Swisher, ed., *Readings on Nathaniel Hawthorne*. San Diego: Greenhaven Press, 1996. Excerpts from four major critics analyze *The Scarlet Letter*'s ambiguity, Old and New England societies, imagery, and artistry.

Carl Van Doren, *The American Novel: 1789–1939*. New York: Macmillan, 1940. The chapter on Hawthorne covers biographical information, argues that the past cannot be shed, and provides the circumstances of the novel writing.

Mark Van Doren, *Nathaniel Hawthorne*. New York: Viking, 1949. The chapter on *The Scarlet Letter* discusses Hester as heroine and other characters as types.

## Puritanism and the History of New England

William Bradford, et al., *Homes in the Wilderness: A Pilgrim's Journal of Plymouth Plantation*. Ed. Margaret Wise Brown. Hamden, CT: Lennet Books, 1988. Gives account of the Pilgrim arrival, building a community, and contact with Indians who helped them.

William Dudley and Teresa O'Neill, *Puritanism: Opposing Viewpoints*. San Diego: Greenhaven Press, 1994. Excerpts covering the Puritan vision, religious dissent, forming a colony, dealings with Native Americans, and the crises of witchcraft.

Max Farrand, ed., *The Laws and Liberties of Massachusetts: Reprinted from the Copy of the 1648 Edition in the Henry E. Huntington Library*. Cambridge, MA: Harvard University Press, 1929. Records laws concerning marriage, protection, justice, weights and measures, and relationships between parents and children.

Rod W. Horton and Herbert W. Edwards, *Backgrounds of American Literary Thought*. New York: Appleton-Century-Crofts, 1952. Explains theological, intellectual, and political thought of New England.

George J. Landevich, comp. and ed., *A Chronological and Documentary History: 1602–1970*. Dobbs Ferry, NY: Oceana Publications, 1974. Chronicles a Puritan town and includes documents from John Winthrop and the trial of Anne Hutchinson.

Mason I. Lowance Jr., *Increase Mather*. New York: Twayne, 1974. A biography of an important New England leader and the way he shaped life, history, science, religion, and politics.

Perry Miller, *The New England Mind: The Seventeenth Century*. Cambridge, MA: Harvard University Press, 1953. A good cultural history covering religion, witchcraft, trade, and social life.

Perry Miller and Thomas H. Johnson, eds., *The Puritans*. New York: American Book, 1936. An extensive collection of Puritan history, religion, social customs, biographies, letters, poetry, education, and science.

# Index

# Picture Credits

Cover Photo: The Granger Collection, New York

© Bettmann/CORBIS, 32

© 1997 N. Carter/North Wind, 31

© E.O. Hoppe/CORBIS, 26

© Hulton/Archive by Getty Images, 9, 15, 37

Library of Congress, 13, 17, 19, 20, 23, 24

North Wind Picture Archives, 28, 29, 34, 40

Photofest, 10, 39, 42, 44, 48, 49, 51, 54, 57, 58, 59, 61, 63, 65, 67, 69, 71, 75

© 2001 Stock Montage, Inc., 21, 46, 64

# About the Author

Clarice Swisher is a freelance writer and editor and a former English teacher. She taught English in Minnesota for several years before devoting full time to writing. She is the author or editor of more than twenty books, including *The Importance of Pablo Picasso, The Glorious Revolution,* and *Genetic Engineering,* published by Lucent Books, and *The Spread of Islam, William Faulkner,* and *John F. Kennedy,* published by Greenhaven Press. She lives in Saint Paul, Minnesota.